Help!
My Little Boy's
Growing Up

Annette Smith

HARVEST HOUSE™ PUBLISHERS

EUGENE, OREGON

Cover by Terry Dugan Design, Minneapolis, Minnesota

Published in association with the literary agency of Alive Communications, Inc., 7680 Goddard Street, Suite 200, Colorado Springs, CO 80920

HELP! MY LITTLE BOY'S GROWING UP
Copyright © 2002 Annette Smith
Published by Harvest House Publishers
Eugene, Oregon 97402

Library of Congress Cataloging-in-Publication Data

Smith, Annette Gail, 1959-
  Help! my little boy's growing up / Annette Smith.
    p. cm.
  ISBN 0-7369-1018-2 (pbk.)
  1. Teenage boys. 2. Parent and teenager. I. Title.
  HQ797 .S53 2002
  649'.132—dc21   2002003619

Printed in the United States of America

  02 03 04 05 06 07 08 09 / VP-MS / 10 9 8 7 6 5 4 3 2 1

Contents

A Note from Annette 7

1. Boy, oh Boy! 9

2. What's Happening Down There? 21

3. Girls Allowed! 31

4. Just Stylin' 43

5. Hittin' the Books 55

6. Don't Kiss Me in Front of My Friends 67

7. Just One of the Guys 79

8. Look, Mom—No Hands! 93

9. God and Me 105

10. Roll 'Em 117

11. Time to Sweat 129

12. Making the Team 141

13. But I'm Broke! 153

14. Like Father, Like Son 165

15. Mama's Boy 177

16. Preparing for Launch 187

Acknowledgments

First, I owe thanks to my adult son, Russell. He graciously allowed me to share stories and details from his growing-up years. Russell's a son who makes his mom proud. He's smart, funny, laid-back, and easy to please.

Every mom I know remembers her mistakes. A few months ago I felt the need to apologize to Russell for the times when he was little and I was too hard on him. I wanted to make verbal amends for the occasions when I disciplined him too harshly.

"Aw, don't worry about it, Mom," he said. "I'm all right. I think I've turned out pretty okay—don't you?"

Yes, Russell. You have definitely turned out okay.

My husband, Randy, has been a great partner to me and a wonderful dad to these children of ours. Though I don't for a minute claim to understand the male half of the species, Randy has given me lots of insight and information about how boys and young men think and feel, and about what drives them to behave the ways that they do.

My daughter, Rachel, is smart and pretty and always makes it home by curfew. Her mature behavior and trustworthy nature make it easy for me to devote big chunks of time to my work.

Thanks to my agent, Chip MacGregor, for helping me succeed in this business of words.

Friends at Harvest House Publishers grow dearer with each passing year. I so appreciate the confidence they place in me. It is a pleasure to work with such pleasant folks.

To God be the glory!

For Lloyd and Dorothy Smith,
who reared the boy
that married me.
Thanks.
You did good!

A Note from Annette

Last year I wrote a book for moms called *Help! My Little Girl's Growing Up.* That little paperback, written to give moms bits of gentle advice and encouragement, was received with lots of enthusiasm. Moms (and dads) told me how much the book helped them understand their adolescent daughters.

"But what about our sons?" those same parents complained. "We need help understanding what's going on with our guys."

"You should write a book about raising boys," they said.

And as you can see, that's what I did.

There is something you should know right off. The ideas expressed in this book are not the words of what we Southerners would call a high-dollar expert. Sure, I'm a registered nurse. I've studied child development, and I've worked with troubled teens. But mostly, I'm just a mom. I'm a mom who loves her son and who, since the day of his birth, has desired more than anything to see him grow up to be a godly man. In the rearing of my now 21-year-old son, Russell, I've made lots of mistakes. But I've also done some things right. For sure, I've learned a bunch along the way.

The topics in this book are the stuff that parents of adolescents discuss with each other while leaning against a counter in someone's kitchen. Moms and dads talk about these things while sitting in folding chairs during halftime breaks of youth soccer games and while sipping fellowship-hall coffee after Sunday night services.

Parents of boys have universal concerns.

If you're a parent of a boy between the ages of 10 and 14, and especially if you're that boy's *mom*, chances are, you're seeing some confusing changes taking place in your son. It seems that he's growing up way too fast.

What's normal?

What's not?

What should make me worry, and what should I ignore?

In the pages of this book, you'll find helpful advice and a few answers to some of these questions. Mostly though, what you're going to find here is hope, humor, and encouragement. Raising an adolescent boy is not a grievous, impossible task. Relax. You can do this. Yes, you *really can*.

And the best part? You're going to have lots of fun!

1
Boy, oh Boy!

Randy and I became engaged while on Christmas break of our last year of college. When we returned to classes in early January, our plans for a spring wedding caused quite a stir among our friends. Even members of the faculty at our small, close-knit school expressed shock. Some of them actually tried to discourage our plans.

Who could blame them? The last time any of them had seen us had been a mere five weeks before—on the afternoon that we had cheerily said our December holiday goodbyes. As of *that* day, Randy and I had both been seriously involved with *other people.*

"When did you two get together?"

"The day after finals."

"But I thought you were going out with…"

"I was. But we broke up."

"And you're really *engaged?*"

"Already?"

"To each other?"

"Uh-huh. Want to see the ring?"

What can I say? We just knew. Some things are meant to be. Our sunny May wedding was a dream come true for us both. We said our vows in my parents' backyard and politely nibbled cake and sipped fruit punch until, at the first acceptable moment, we escaped into our balloon-filled red Chevy and burned rubber toward a three-day San Antonio honeymoon.

We weren't just anxious to begin our honeymoon. Having just graduated, Randy and I were eager to begin our adult lives. We couldn't get started fast enough. Such big plans we two had! First, we would establish our careers. Then we would save some money—enough for a down payment on a house. Along the way, we would do some traveling, invest in hobbies—art lessons for me, golf for Randy—and spend lots of time with our friends.

Children?

Some day, of course. But not for a while. A *long* while, we agreed.

Shortly after our wedding, I sat perched on a folding chair in a young women's Bible class at our church. The teacher, a sweet-faced older woman (looking back, I realize she likely wasn't a day over 45) explained to us that many women in the Bible gave birth to many children. Giving us a cute wink and displaying the slightest of pink blushes, the teacher continued. "They didn't have the option, like you young women do today, of spacing out their pregnancies and planning the number of children they would have."

Being the only member of the class who was not yet a mother, I didn't understand why her words prompted snickers and elbow jabs—even a few outright guffaws in six of the 15 class members present.

I was soon to find out.

"But how?" asked Randy on the morning that I told him.

"I don't know," I said.

"Are you *sure?*"

"No. But I'll find out tomorrow."

I found two things out on that "tomorrow." The first one was something that those snickering mothers and mothers-to-be already knew. No method of family planning is a sure thing! The second was that our lives as a couple were about to change.

It's a Boy!

Oh, how they changed! Four months before our second anniversary, a laid-back, chubby-cheeked little guy came to live at our house. He was born at straight up noon—the time of day when the sun is at its brightest. We named him Russell after a boy I had a crush on when I was in the third grade, and we gave him the middle name David in honor of Randy's grandfather on his mother's side.

That little guy, the one whose early existence surprised his dad and me, was our firstborn son. He turned 21 years old this week. I baked him his favorite cake—chocolate from a mix—and took him shopping for new shoes. His dad, in keeping with a tradition he started when Russell was eight, treated him to dinner out and a professional basketball game.

According to the law in our state, Russell's a man now—able to vote, get drafted, and hold public office. Oh yes, and not to forget, "drink beer," he reminds me in a futile attempt to get my goat. Is he too big to spank? I fear so!

A man. I still find it hard to believe.

It Happens So Fast

Most dads and moms, like my husband and me, are startled at how rapidly their little boys begin that transition from children into men. It comes as a shock when we realize that suddenly, instead of Velcro tennies, he's wearing size-10 Dr. Martens…and needing size 11!

There's the scraggly beginnings of a goatee where our son's three cute little baby chins used to be. And his upper lip? That's not chocolate milk.

Even though he still manages to hit the dirty clothes hamper with his socks less than 20 percent of the time, he can actually make a basket at a real hoop in a gym. When did he get to be so tall? Who taught him to jump so high?

His jokes are actually funny. Some of them are even funnier than ours. He can do impressions. Of us. He cracks his granddad up.

Some of this growing-up stuff is entertaining and fun. Some of it we fight. More than one mom I know dug their heels in when it came to their son's sudden interest in girls. Few dads relish the idea of teaching their son to drive the family van. No one wants to deal with a boy learning to play the trumpet; fewer still with one who has a steely determination to see exactly how the insides of the family's VCR works.

But it happens. All this and more, just as God intended it. Boys this age sprout up and out in all directions—physically, mentally, emotionally, and spiritually. If you've got a son between the ages of 10 and 13, look out! You're in for all this stuff and more.

They're Not the Same as Their Sisters

Here's a hint that parents of kids of both sexes already know: Little boys are different from little girls—and in more ways than just that diaper-dodging thing! Their rearing presents unique challenges. Their growth from boys into men is different from girls' growth into women. Dads know this. Some moms may not.

Most of my women friends admit that they don't really understand men. Few women think that they do. This puts us at a disadvantage when it comes to rearing our boys. No matter how much we love and care for our sons, we can never completely understand what our boys are experiencing as they grow to be men. It's extremely helpful for all moms, and especially single moms, to spend time talking to men about their adolescence. Ask them how they related to their families and peers. What was most difficult about those years? What was most fun?

Several traits stand out as being distinctly male. Boys are by nature more aggressive than their sisters. They have a greater need to dominate and to conquer, to push and test parental limits. They are also much more prone to take risks. Though these traits will manifest themselves in various ways according to a boy's personality, temperament, and interests, they will be increasingly noticeable as your son nears adolescence. These traits are *normal* and should be directed and channeled, not eliminated or changed.

In some ways, raising boys is easier than raising girls. In some ways, it's more difficult. Neither is better, neither is worse. They're just different. That's the way God made them—and aren't we glad! Sure keeps things interesting!

They're All Unique

Sons come in all shapes and sizes with various talents, interests, temperaments, and aptitudes. The greatest overall challenge for parents of boys ages 10 to 14—for it is usually between those ages that boys begin to make their way through the puzzling maze of adolescence—is to guide them as they grow to be the men God intends them to be. As parents it's our task not only to love our boys, but to know them individually—to be familiar with their strengths, their weaknesses, their dreams, and their fears.

To pigeonhole all boys, to assume that they are all alike—rowdy and loud, athletic and prow—or to speak about them in general terms as if they are all interested in randomly tearing stuff up and in making big messes, is to ignore the ones who are quiet or have laid-back, easygoing temperaments. Many boys (future engineers, perhaps?) are careful and deliberate in their actions. Many others are sensitive, musical, or artistic, and they are as normal and male as they can be.

God made each boy different from every other boy on earth. It's when we accept our sons for who and how God made them, when we love and affirm them just as they are, that they're open to our guidance, which they desperately need during this transitional time.

Be Positive

The truth is, raising an adolescent boy can be a ton of fun. Contrary to some of the messages current media would have us believe, the rearing of healthy, happy, well-behaved boys is not an impossible task. Testosterone is not toxic, and puberty is not a prescription for disaster. Don't get locked into fear or dread of these adolescent years.

While seatbelts are encouraged and knee pads are suggested (due to the increased amount of time parents of adolescent boys are prompted to spend in prayer), parental helmets are optional. Heads up! Most moms, dads, and sons make it through with no more than a few bumps and bruises.

Some Real Concerns

There *are* some truly tricky times that parents face as their boys reach adolescence. Some boys and their parents *do* have a rough time during the transition. Maybe you're worried about drugs and alcohol, sex, gangs, and criminal behavior. You've read statistics about teenage rebellion and the dangerous ways some boys act out. Perhaps you have friends or family members whose boys have given them lots of grief. It's easy to expect troubled times ahead.

Like most parents of boys, I received many grave warnings as Russell approached adolescence (some of them from folks who didn't even have kids).

My friend Dee Phillips, who's a jovial father of four grown children—two of whom were rowdy boys—jokingly told me when he learned I was expecting a baby that if I had a son, for his protection *and* mine, I should immediately put the child in a wooden box with a lid. Once in a while, it would be a good idea to open the lid and slip some food and water inside. However, he said, when that son hit 13, I should nail the lid shut and not open it until he turned 20.

Most Turn Out Just Fine

While it's true there are no perfect sons and—guess what!—no perfect parents, *most* boys go through adolescence without major problems. Most boys *don't* do drugs, join gangs, or get their girlfriends pregnant. Most boys love and respect their parents. They go to school, do their chores, have a good time with their friends, and grow up to be just fine.

Expect the best. Look for the good times. Shrug off the predictions of people who think all boys must go through dangerously rebellious and difficult times in order to become men. Be wise, not naive, but prepare to deal with problems only if and when they come up.

Let's Hear It for Boys!

Sounds crazy, but in today's politically correct climate, boys need to be told that being a male is a very good thing. They need to hear affirming words, not once, not twice, but over and over again.

They may hear things that make them feel as though their very maleness is something that needs to be fixed, treated, tamed, or trained out of them—as if that were possible! Even our favorite family-friendly television shows often portray male characters to be physically, mentally, and morally inferior to female characters. Male bashing is a common comedic theme. The down-with-men message is in some measure a response to problems of equality faced by women and girls, but society suffers when one group exalts itself by pushing another group down.

It's easy for us moms to subconsciously allow negative beliefs about males to creep into our thought patterns and our conversations. Guard against doing so. Our boys pick up such messages as if by radar. If sons believe that they are expected to behave in crude, violent, insensitive, socially unacceptable ways, they will live up to those expectations.

Instead, our sons need to receive, *loud and clear*, the message that being a boy who will soon be a man is a good thing—a *wonderful* thing. They need to see and hear that men are responsible, kind, and strong. Men can achieve. Men are husbands and dads, workers and teachers, friends and coaches. Being a man means you can have fun, play fair, work hard, and try to make life better for the people around you.

Celebrate the Blessing of a Son

On a shelf in my office sits a three-inch-high ceramic pig. It's a girl pig. I know so because despite her grinning, unladylike pose—she's lying on her back with her feet stuck up in the air like she's peddling a bicycle—she is wearing a cute little ruffled skirt, and she has a bow in her hair. My children and I have enjoyed her so long that she's had her head broken off three times. Thanks to the wonders of superglue, unless you look really close, you can hardly tell.

My friend Vicki, already the mother of two, was with me the exact minute when, via a pre-home-pregnancy-test phone call to the doctor's office, I learned that I was indeed going to have a baby—a baby that would turn out to be Russell. She was so excited that I forgot to be afraid, so enthusiastic about what lay ahead for me that it slipped from my mind that Randy and I had planned to wait several years before starting our family.

We were going to have a baby!

I told Randy the minute he got home from work.

"You really are? You mean we really are?"

"Really."

Once he recovered from the shock, he too, was tickled at the thought of a baby. After spending a couple of hours holding hands on the couch and talking about the unexpected news, we decided to celebrate by going out to eat. It was when we opened the door of our apartment to go out that we found the goodies left there by our friend Vicki.

Next to a pretty green plant in a wicker basket was the happy little ceramic pig—wrapped up in a pretty box. The following note was attached.

> *Congratulations! Someday you can tell your baby that this is how we all felt when we learned he was coming!*
>
> *Love, Vicki*

When I think of what fun it's been having this son of mine—the little fellow who started out as such a surprise to his dad and me—I feel as happy as that little ceramic pig looks.

How did we feel when we learned he was coming?

The same way that I feel today—like the most blessed woman on earth.

Sons are a heritage from the LORD,
children a reward from him.

—PSALM 127:3

Ways to Affirm that It's Great to Be a Guy

1. After calling ahead for permission, take your son to visit your local fire station. Bring brownies or cookies as a gesture of appreciation for the job that the firefighters do. Explain to your son that while a few women are firefighters, because of the physical strength and agility required to do the job, firefighting is a career dominated by men.

2. When the newspaper prints articles about men who have shown exceptional courage, who have behaved in unusually honorable ways, or who have sacrificed time or money for the good of others, clip them out for your son.

3. Play games regularly with your son. Ask him to show you how to play his favorite computer game. Initiate tick-tack-toe games when you have to wait at the doctor or dentist's office. Engage him in word games when traveling together in the car.

4. On gift occasions, give your son biographies of famous men.

5. Teach him manners. Explain that it's polite for a man to offer his seat to a woman, to allow her to walk first, and to open the door for her in social situations.

2
What's Happening Down There?

When Russell was in the fifth grade, I received a call from one of my friends who had a son in the same class. "I was surprised you weren't at the meeting at school today," she said.

"What meeting?" I asked.

"You know. The one on AIDS. Didn't you get the note?"

No, I hadn't gotten the note—the one informing parents of the special meeting, the one inviting them to come and be a part of the class, to ask questions of the public health nurse who was coming to address what, 15 years ago, was a new and unfamiliar topic.

The minute Russell got into the car that afternoon, I pounced. "What's this I hear about a special meeting at school?"

He turned eight shades of red. Purple too, as I recall.

"How come I didn't get the note?"

"I was afraid you'd come," Russell mumbled. He stared out the window, guilty and caught.

I mulled this over. He was right. Of course—I *would* have come. Absolutely. No way would I have missed a meeting at my son's public school at which sex was the planned topic of discussion. Thanks to not getting the note, it was too late now.

"So," I said, both hands on the wheel. "They talked to you about AIDS."

"Yes." He pressed his forehead against the glass.

"Do you know what AIDS is?"

"Uh-huh." He scratched his nose.

"Did the nurse explain to you the different ways that a person can get it?"

"Yes." Russell slumped down in his seat.

"*All* of the ways?"

"Yes." I detected a groan.

"Did you understand everything that she said?"

"Yes." He lowered his chin in an attempt to draw his head down into his coat. We had a pet turtle one time that would do the same thing when he was trying to get away from something frightening or unpleasant.

"Do you have any questions?"

"No." He wiped his palms on his pants.

"Are you sure?"

"Yes." Then before I could say anything else, he pleaded, "Mom, could we *please* talk about something else?"

Russell's hesitancy to talk to me—his mother—about a sexual matter such as the transmission of AIDS isn't unusual. Boys on the threshold of puberty are both eager for information and reluctant to seek it.

Puberty's the Real Name of the Game

Let's be honest. When it comes to raising boys, few words strike universal fear and anxiety in the hearts of parents as does the term *puberty*.

Moms and dads have lots of questions about this phase of their sons' growth and development. Parents wonder, *What exactly is puberty? What causes it? When does it start? How long does it last? What does a son need to know?* Moms especially feel unprepared for this phase of their sons' lives. Sons, though they won't likely bring it up, feel anxious about body changes too. It's not knowing what's ahead that makes the transition more difficult for everyone.

Puberty is simply the word we use to describe the time period (years) during which a boy's body moves from that of a child into that of a man capable of producing a child. The changes that you are seeing now—or that you will soon see—are occurring exactly the way God planned. His design is perfect. Though it may appear that hormones have caused your son to go haywire, an adolescent boy's body is not broken. It does not need to be fixed. These are exciting years, because it's now that we begin to see a glimmer of the man that our son is going to be.

Sorry, Mom

When their bodies start to change, boys need information. They have lots of questions. They worry about themselves and wonder if they are normal. However, no matter how much they need facts, they are likely to be terribly embarrassed to talk about such concerns with anyone— especially with their moms. Most moms can get away with addressing basic gender-neutral topics like voice changes, body odor, and acne, but nearly all boys most emphatically *do not* care to discuss with their mother any of those matters taking place further south than their armpits.

Dad is the best person to discuss puberty and sex with a son. A boy will naturally identify with his dad as his body becomes more like that of a man. In some families Dad's either not available or not up to the task. When that's the case, Mom can arrange for a grandfather, an uncle, or a trusted family friend to explain things. Be sure whoever is chosen is someone who can be counted on to spend regular time with your son. He will have other concerns and other questions that he'll need to have answered.

Let's face it. Some of this stuff is embarrassing for us *and* for our boys. It's tempting to ignore the changes and to let all of this slide.

Don't.

For though he's likely to glean much more information on his own than his parents are aware of or would prefer, *no* adolescent boy should be left to learn about his changing body from his peers, from the media, or even from his health teacher at school.

The Basics

Testosterone is the hormonal catalyst that determines the sex of the baby. It's the force that catapults ours sons from boyhood into manhood. Testosterone is powerful stuff. Sometime between the ages of 10 and 14, through a chain of events set into motion by the pituitary gland, a boy's "testosterone switch" gets flipped on, triggering a predictable chain of developmental events. Not until he's 16 to 18 years of age will the process be mostly complete.

The age of the onset of puberty varies from boy to boy, and our sons feel a gripping anxiety if they begin their development later than their friends do. These boys need to be reassured that they are normal and that they will develop in due time. If Dad was a late bloomer, his son may be one too.

Sons who experience puberty's onset earlier than their peers face increased pressures too. Their bodies look mature, but their brains may lag years behind. Expecting too much emotional maturity of 12-year-old guys who happen to look 16 can cause problems.

Both sets of boys, the ones who hit puberty early and the ones who develop at a later age, need parental love, support, and the reassurance that they are developing exactly as they should.

High-Water Jeans and Hungry 24/7

Next time you're in the grocery store, notice the woman whose cart is overflowing, the one stocking up on what looks to be enough cereal, milk, bread, bananas, cheap generic cookies, and ground beef to feed a small country. If you think she's laying up enough food for a week, think again. If she's got an adolescent boy at home, she's hoping to make it through three days before she comes back for more.

The average adolescent boy will nearly *double* his weight between the ages of 12 and 16. His height may increase by four or more inches a year. No wonder he's always hungry! Don't be surprised when he gets up from the dinner table, goes to the pantry, and starts rummaging around for a snack.

The notorious adolescent growth spurt is among the first signs of puberty. Curious as to when it will occur? Here's a hint. Keep an eye on your son's hands and feet. When they start to grow, look out. The rest of him is sure to follow. He will also develop a broader chest and a more muscular trunk and shoulders. Your son will seem to shoot up overnight and may go through three sizes of jeans in six months or less. The phrase "can't walk and chew gum at the same time" comes to mind as well.

What Else?

Ask any mom. She'll tell you that most little boys, especially after they've been outside playing, smell a lot like puppies. Neither puppies nor little boys smell particularly *great,* but neither do they reek. In early adolescence that changes. Skipping baths is no longer an option. Sweat glands become active, and the boys attached to those glands need deodorant. Be firm but nonchalant and relaxed about the need for increased attention to hygiene. Purchase the same brand of deodorant that Dad uses. Suggest that now would be a good time for him to start applying it after every shower.

Many boys this age become conscious of the benefits of smelling good. They discover their dad's cologne or may be given some of their own. Believing that more has got to be better than less, adolescents tend to bathe in it. To avoid becoming overcome in the car on the way to church when riding with such a boy, parents, for their own protection, can explain that just a dab will do.

Some boys this age are plagued with acne. Explain to your son that keeping his face clean is important. If he has pimples, purchase over-the-counter acne medications and explain to him how to use them. If the problem persists, is terribly noticeable, bothers him a great deal, or is painful, consult a dermatologist.

Voice changes occur about midway through the transition. Expect his voice to deepen, crack, and vary in pitch. Boys whose voices have already changed get a kick when someone calls and mistakes them for their dad. Other boys are less thrilled when, despite feeling like they are becoming manly type men, a caller mistakes them for their younger sister.

Other Stuff

Early in adolescence a boy will begin to notice that he now has pubic hair. Later he'll grow hair under his arms, followed even later by the beginnings of a mustache and beard. His genitals will grow to adult size, and he may experience nocturnal emissions, also called "wet dreams." It's a good idea for boys to be given the occasional responsibility of doing their own laundry when the first signs of adolescence appear. That way, should the need arise, he can easily launder his own sheets or underwear without calling unwanted attention to what, for him, will be an embarrassing situation.

Understandably and appropriately, a son whose body is beginning to look more like a man's than a child's is going to be increasingly modest. It's important that parents—and under their direction, siblings—respect and provide for his increased need for privacy.

Knock Before Entering

Few topics make parents as uncomfortable as does masturbation. Is it morally wrong? Should they talk about it with their sons? Most experts, both Christian and secular, believe that masturbation is an almost universal experience for adolescents. While some Christians believe that it's wrong, many do not.

One mom I know handled the topic like this: When her son was getting close to school age, she noticed that often, when he was lying on the floor watching television, he would have his hand inside his pants. Without making a big deal of the situation, she explained, "Touching your private parts feels good. Everybody does it. Everybody also picks their nose. Just like picking your nose, touching your private parts is something you need to do when you are alone. When you want to touch yourself there, you need to go into the bathroom and close the door. Understand?" He did. She did not bring the subject up with him ever again.

Whether masturbation is a moral issue or is not is something that should be prayerfully determined by individual parents. Whatever you decide to tell or not tell your son about masturbation, it's of the greatest importance that he understand that he is loved and accepted by God no matter what. Teens who feel guilty about masturbation may believe that they are unacceptable to Him if they try to abstain and are unsuccessful. Be sure your son understands that God's grace and love and forgiveness covers *every* area of his life.

He's Normal and He's Great!

The physical signs of growth that you see in your adolescent son are simply outward signals of inside changes. As you watch your little boy begin to inhabit the body of a man, know that he is growing and developing just as he should. God made him strong and healthy, rambunctious and active. Enjoy him!

> *Thank you for making me so wonderfully complex!*
> *It is amazing to think about.*
> *Your workmanship is marvelous—and how well I know it.*

—PSALM 139:14 TLB

Growing-Up-Guy Stuff

1. Boys love it when they grow to be taller than their mothers. On the day that he first notices that he's passed Mom up, mark it on the calendar, then bake a cake or go out for ice cream. Celebrate in some silly or fun way.

2. Use his strength. Ask him to open the pickle jar lid that's on too tight. Request his help when moving furniture. Tell him that having someone around who can help with tough jobs is great.

3. When his voice has changed to the point that he no longer gets surprised by cracks and squeaks, ask him to record the message on the family's answering machine. Don't be surprised if he calls home just to hear himself.

4. When a shadow appears on his upper lip, buy him the same kind of razor and shaving cream Dad uses.

3
Girls Allowed!

It was a big day for Russell. Earlier in the month he'd turned 16. To honor the occasion, we'd had a family party. He'd gotten presents, and I'd baked a cake. His dad, in keeping with a birthday tradition started when he was eight years old, had treated him to a guys-only dinner out and tickets to a professional basketball game.

For all of our celebratory efforts Russell had said thanks. Thanks a lot, in fact. He had gobbled up his cake and torn into his presents. He had obviously relished the meal alone with his dad, and he had yelled and cheered for his favorite pro basketball team, the Dallas Mavericks.

We were pleased at our son's mannerly response, but not surprised. Our Russell is a polite guy, one who is quick to show his appreciation for the things we do for him.

However, from his dad's and my observations, every one of the efforts we had made to give him a good birthday paled in comparison to *this* day's planned outing. Russell was pumped—as excited as I could remember seeing him since his first day of T-ball back when he was five.

"Can we go yet?" Standing with his hand on the front door of our house, he bounced from one foot to the other. "Are you ready, Mom? Can we go, Dad? They close at five."

It was one o'clock.

Torturing him, Randy and I dragged our feet. "I don't know. Looks like it might rain. Think we ought to wait until tomorrow?" I said.

"Maybe. Let me take a look at the sky," said Randy.

"Mom! No!" Russell protested. "Can we please go now? *Please?*"

So where, exactly, was Russell so eager to go? Why was our normally tardy son nudging his dad and me so hurriedly towards the door? What was the day's planned destination?

It wasn't to an amusement park, a movie theater, or an arcade to which Russell wanted to go, but to an out-of-the-way, ugly, gray-brick state government building. Yep. That's the one—the Texas Department of Motor Vehicles, known to Russell and all of his about-to-turn-16 friends as the Driver's License Place.

We made it there in plenty of time, and Russell passed his driving test with flying colors. When he was done, he toed the taped line, grinned like a Cheshire cat for the driver's license camera, and signed his name on the line. Whoopee! This was the day he had waited for since he could remember. Even though he would be sharing a decidedly *uncool* baby blue Chevy station wagon with me, nothing could take away from the exultation he felt at finally being allowed to drive. Finally, he could drive himself to school. Or get a job if he wanted. Or run to the store when he thirsted for a soda. Or take himself and his friends to the movies, to church, and to basketball games.

Oh, and one other thing…now he could date. Girls. Whenever he wanted.

Soon as he could get one to say yes.

Russell was self-confident and sure of himself in every area except for one—asking girls out. He, like most guys, was afraid that they might tell him no.

"So what?" I said. "You just ask another one if the first girl says no. No big deal."

His dad, who remembered what it was like to be a dating-age young man, understood why Russell rolled his eyes at my flippant comments. "You don't know what it's like, Annette. It's hard to be the guy."

"No pain, no gain," I said. "Besides, guys are the ones who have it easy. Girls have to sit around and *wait* for someone to call them and ask them out."

Unwilling to validate my comments with a reply, Russell rolled his eyes. Randy hid his behind his newspaper.

Okay. Maybe I don't get it.

It took him a few months, but Russell finally decided on Kelly, a cute girl he knew from school who had sparkly dark eyes and silky brown hair. She would be the one—the woman he would take out on his very first real date.

He called her up. They talked. Russell asked if she would like to do something come Friday night.

So far so good. She said yes. I was pleased. Kelly was a sweet girl. I knew her mom and dad. They were a Christian family who shared our values. Who better to be our son's first date?

In preparation for their date, Russell washed the car. He had been saving his money, planning what they would do. First, out to eat. Then a movie. Maybe he and Kelly would stop for ice cream on the way home. On the night of the date he took extra long in the bathroom. When he came out he smelled good. He looked good too. Even his sister said so.

Finally, it was time for him to go pick her up. "Did you brush your teeth?" I teased. "Don't forget to open the car door for her. And remember to put your napkin in your lap."

"Mom!" Russell shrugged me off.

"Have fun!" his dad, his sister, and I called as he left.

Five minutes before midnight, I heard the sound of the baby blue station wagon pulling up into the driveway of our house. Excellent. Russell had made it home by curfew. When he came into the house, feigning nonchalance from my spot on the couch, I yawned and stretched. Randy had already gone to bed.

"Hey there. How did it go?"

"Good. We had fun."

"Great! Everything went okay?"

"Yeah."

"Think you'll ask her out again?"

"No. Probably not."

"How come?"

"Kelly used the 'F' word."

My mouth dropped open and I sprang from the couch. "The 'F' word! Russell! She didn't! Kelly? Kelly said the 'F' word? Why, I would have never guessed anything like that of her. I thought she was a good Christian girl!"

"She is," said Russell.

Well. I could see right now that Russell and I were going to have to have us a nice little talk if he thought that it was acceptable for good Christian girls to talk like that.

"Mom, she said that she wants to be friends."

Friends? Oh. *That* "F" word.

"Russell!"

"Had you going there, didn't I, Mom?" He plopped down on the couch.

I tossed a pillow at him and just missed his head. "Yes, you did. Are you disappointed?"

"No, not really. We had a good time anyway. It just wasn't what I thought it was gonna be. I'm okay. Goodnight, Mom. See you in the morning."

That was half a dozen years ago. Russell, who's now 21, still considers Kelly a friend. Even though the evening didn't turn out like he'd hoped, I'm glad that his first date was with her. Happily, though he's yet to find the girl of his dreams, Russell has gone on to enjoy the company of quite a few young ladies who did not use the dreaded "F" word at all.

Girls Aren't So Gross Anymore

The transformation will be amazing. It will likely take you by surprise. One day a son avoids even brushing against the girls in his class for fear of catching "girl germs." He makes gagging sounds when he sees kissing on TV. A week later, he's passing notes to a girl in his class, sneaking peeks at the underwear ads in the Sunday newspaper, and trying to figure out what mousse is supposed to do for his hair.

When we noticed the change in Russell, it was hard not to tease. The evening that I caught on that he'd been on the phone talking to a girl for the first time, he blushed. I gave him a hug. "Don't be embarrassed. Your dad and I are *glad* that you like *girls. Really.*"

"Mom!"

Just like every other phase of development, boys become interested in girls at a variety of ages. Some ten-year-olds are already saving their allowances to buy boxes of candy for their valentine sweethearts. A few 14-year-olds haven't given girls second thoughts. Both boys are normal. They need for us to affirm that they are. They need to know that when the time is right, they will enjoy spending time with girls—but that there is a lot of other fun stuff to do in the meantime.

Dating?

In a word—no. Not for a while. While crushes and flirtations are normal and harmless, young boys are not ready for real pairings off. Sure, parents of seventh graders may hear that their sons are "going with someone," "going out," or "going steady," depending on the local teen jargon. If you hear such, should you be concerned? Not likely. None of this "going" actually amounts to much—unless you count trips to the water fountain, the band hall, or to the devotional in the parking lot after Sunday evening church.

Yet a word of caution. Parents of adolescents, especially boys, can find themselves easily cajoled into driving their son and his "girlfriend" to the movies or skating. All fixed up, giggling and awkward at age 12 or 13, they look so cute! Why not give them a ride? Many parents see nothing wrong with the practice. Some even encourage it. The problem is that boys and girls this age are still *children.* Dating—and that's exactly what it is, even with parents in tow—is not an appropriate activity for children. It's our job as parents to provide our children with experiences that enhance these developing years and to shield them from experiences they are not yet ready for.

Kids this age have crushes. Infatuations are normal. The wise parent doesn't worry about them too much, but handles the news of a son's girlfriend by expressing only mild interest. On the occasion that you learn that he has a first girlfriend, use the time to casually mention what family rules about dating will be, discuss telephone guidelines, and talk about the importance of treating girls kindly and with respect. Tell him that while it's great that he likes a girl, there will be plenty of time for serious relationships when he gets older.

Here's a sampling of dating guidelines we've used in our family. Some of these ideas may be more lenient than what you feel is right for your family. Some of them may sound unnecessarily strict. We have bent a few of these rules when circumstances seemed to merit doing so. Adapt them to your family and your teen. Use them as a starting place for parental discussions about how you will handle your son's dating experiences.

Smith Family Dating Rules

1. No individual "car" dates before age 16.

2. We must know where you will be at all times. If your plans change or you will be home later than the time we've agreed upon, we expect a call. (Cell phones are great. I highly recommend them for parents of semi-independent kids. Having one takes away the age-old excuse, "I would have called but I couldn't find a phone.")

3. No dating anyone more than two grades ahead or two grades behind.

4. No more than one "alone" date per week. Church activities, group dates, and parties are not included.

5. You may go to a girl's house or she may visit in our home one evening a week, but only if a parent is present in the house.

Discussing the family dating rules ahead of time is a good idea. Time passes quickly, and soon your son *will* be allowed to go out with girls! Keep in mind that interest in the opposite sex is a good and healthy thing. Such interest just shouldn't occupy too much of the 10- to 14-year-old's time.

Boys who are busy with lots of activities tend to be less interested in girls than boys who are lonely and bored. Encourage your son's friendships with other guys. Should you be in the mood to play chauffeur, haul a bunch of boys to the miniature golf course, a high school baseball game, or out to eat pizza after church. If girls mysteriously show up at the same place—fine. Nothing wrong with kids having fun together.

Just not on dates.

Yet.

Phone's for Him

As a general rule, adolescent girls become interested in boys at an earlier age than boys become interested in girls. Almost without exception, adolescent girls *love* to talk on the phone. Most parents of boys will at some point find themselves faced with the problem of girls who call their sons on the phone.

A lot.

It used to be unacceptable for girls to call boys. No longer is that the case. Whether that change is a good one or not could be debated. The fact is, these days girls do their fair share of dialing up.

What's a parent to do about girls, or one particular girl, who calls five, six, seven, or more times a day? She interrupts family mealtimes, homework, and sleep. She's getting on our nerves, and our son doesn't even act like he wants to talk to her. Handling a problem when the situation is the result of the behavior of someone *else's* child can be sticky.

First, decide the amount of phone time tolerable for your household. What do *you* consider to be acceptable phone use? Rules can go both ways. Here's a sampling of guidelines other parents have effectively used:

Family Phone Rules

1. No calls after 9:00 P.M. on school nights, 10:30 P.M. on weekends.

2. No calling the same person more than two times in one day.

3. Phone calls must be limited to 15 minutes. No more than 45 minutes of phone time allowed per day.

4. No calling and hanging up.

5. If the person you are calling is not at home, leave a message. Wait for her to call you back.

If your family has a problem with incoming phone calls, ask your son to explain the rules to the caller himself. This saves embarrassment for the son as well as the girl making the calls. If the problem persists, Mom or Dad should answer the phone and explain the rules to the caller. Inform her that if she continues to break the rules, your son will not be allowed to take her calls. Be firm and consistent, but kind, realizing that many children are making calls when no parent is at home.

What's the Plan?

We all want our sons to grow up, get married, and become attentive and loving husbands to their wives. When they were younger, that experience seemed far off in the future. Watching our sons change and begin to show real interest in girls reminds us that they are already well on their way to becoming men—husbands and fathers. The dramatic changes that we see taking place in their bodies *and* in their hearts are orchestrated by God to prepare them to do just that.

The examples we set for our sons will guide them as they choose their mates and as they decide what kind of husbands they will be. Parents, dads especially, are with every word and action teaching their sons how to behave in a romantic relationship. The way a son sees his parents treat each other will determine to a great extent the way he will treat his future wife and expect her to treat him.

Not every boy has a mom and dad who have a good relationship. Divorce and unhappy marriages are facts for many families, and there are no perfect husbands or wives. In difficult situations parents will need to talk more, do lots of listening, and explaining as much as is appropriate. Even in less-than-ideal situations, parents can have great and positive influences on their sons.

Hard as it is to believe, soon these goofy young guys of ours, the ones who are pretty scared of the girls that they like, will have grown into confident, sure-of-themselves young men. My advice? Sit back and enjoy watching as the transformation unfolds. Before you know it, you'll be watching *him* as he watches *her* come down the aisle.

> *There are three things too wonderful*
> *for me to understand—no, four!*
> *How an eagle glides through the sky.*
> *How a serpent crawls upon a rock.*
> *How a ship finds its way across the heaving ocean.*
> *The growth of love between a man and a girl.*
>
> —Proverbs 30:18-19 (TLB)

Guys and Gals

1. Encourage your son to invite groups of friends, both boys and girls, into your home. Provide something active for them to do, such as volleyball and s'mores outside if the weather is nice, board games and hot dogs inside if it's wet or cold.

2. Orchestrate time for your son to spend an evening alone with Mom. While calling it a mother-son date would most likely make him gag, arrange for it to be just such. Make the time special by going out to eat and see a movie, taking a hike in the woods, or going to a concert or sporting event. The object of the outing? Fun! Spending time alone with Mom helps him understand females in a way that will be helpful to him when he begins to spend one-on-one time with girls.

3. When watching a video or TV program together, point out situations where a male character is behaving appropriately towards a female character. Discuss times when he is displaying honor, respect, strong character, and restraint. Talk about the consequences of both appropriate and inappropriate behaviors.

4
Just Stylin'

In some ways, little boys are a lot like cats. Both species prefer food they can play with, and neither of them takes to water very well.

I am the oldest of my parents' three children. The only girl, I was blessed with twin brothers four years younger than me. Our growing-up years were spent riding horses, wading in the creek, climbing trees, and crafting home-made playhouses on my dad's multi-acre Texas cattle ranch. We were blessed with happy-go-lucky early childhood years. Being basically compliant and obedient kids, the three of us enjoyed long afternoons of run-of-the-place rural freedom.

Remember the line from the song "Home on the Range"—the one that goes "Where never is heard a discouraging word"? That phrase pretty much describes the childhoods that my little brothers and I enjoyed. Our parents were clear about their expectations for us and we gave them little grief.

Except for over one thing.

Bath time. Both of my brothers hated it.

I remember my mother had to *force* both of their rusty-necked selves into the tub. Left on their own, I don't know if they would have *ever* chosen to take a bath. One of them even got an award at church camp the year he turned ten. It was the Went the Longest Without Taking a Shower award and was presented by the camp's director in a moving, end-of-the-week awards ceremony. In place of a gold medal they gave him a bar of fragrant Dial Soap-On-A-Rope.

His aromatic accomplishment made my mother so very proud.

But then she could have predicted that he would win. So bad were both her boys at skipping their nightly washings that she took to checking the bathtub for rings and feeling the bar of bath soap to see if it was wet. On more than one occasion she discovered dirty brown water-level lines on my brothers' round tummies, telltale signs that while they had, as they claimed, gotten into the water-filled tub, not a drop of the liquid had made contact with their dusty, bone-dry upper bodies.

Back into the tub they would go.

Take a Number

While parents of smelly little boys with grimy fingernails dream of the day that their sons will stop loathing clean skin, few are prepared for their boys' sudden adolescent attraction to water. The change can make a parent wonder where their milk-mustached son has gone. Captured by aliens? Kidnapped by the neighbors who always thought he was cute? One would think.

Here's how to know when your son has crossed over. His transformation from Pig Pen into Mr. Clean will be manifested by markedly higher water bills, a chilling shortage of *hot* water, and an astounding increase in the number of wet towels left on the floor. (One for the head, one for the body, and one for each foot—as best I can tell.)

It's the absolute truth. Once they decide that looking good and smelling nice is important, boys can spend as much or more time in the bathroom as do their sisters. Don't be surprised if your son takes two or more showers a day. He'll shampoo his hair every day, and should he discover hair gel or mousse, go ahead and add a new hair care category to the family budget. As for deodorant? Parents of boys may as well buy half a dozen cans at a time.

This boy will begin to *live* in the bathroom.

Gotta Have the Right Jeans

Sweat pants or ratty jeans and T-shirts used to be all he wanted to wear. If you brought it home in a sack, it was fine by him. No more. Now that he's an adolescent, expect your son to have a great deal to say about his clothes.

Most boys want to fit in with a certain group at school. And different groups adhere to different uniforms. It will be of the utmost importance for a boy's clothes to be exactly like those of the members of the group he admires most. Unfortunately, when he complains that if he wears the wrong clothes he won't be accepted by the group, he may be telling the truth. Parents and sons must decide together how to handle the situation.

Discuss the family's clothing budget with your son. If he is set on having a certain pair of boots, sneakers, or jeans, discuss how he can get them. Maybe he would rather have three pairs of the right jeans than five pairs of the less-desirable ones. Perhaps he would want to spend his birthday money on clothing instead of on video games. Even when his requests seem unreasonable, listen to his point of view. Encourage him to come up with a plan that is acceptable to you and workable for him.

There are other boys, like our son Russell, who will wear anything to avoid looking like everyone else. These guys go to the extreme. Their fashion goal seems to be to dress in shocking ways that embarrass their siblings. (An orange polyester Hawaiian shirt paired with knee-high red-and-white socks—striped à la *The Cat in the Hat*—come to mind.) Being different and standing out are what matter to these boys. They wouldn't be caught dead in designer labels. Thrift shops are their favorite clothing sources.

Adolescent fashion is fickle. What is coveted today may be scorned next week. My friend Marty was tickled when she snagged a pair of expensive designer jeans on sale. She was sure that her son would be overjoyed at receiving them. After all, he had longed for the jeans but been denied them because of their cost. Marty was flabbergasted when he didn't wear them—not even once. Seems the jeans had triple stitching down the side. No one wore that kind of jeans anymore. This week the right jeans were a pair with double stitching. Double or nothing. His mother chose *nothing*.

Hair or There

A peek into my husband Randy's high school yearbook reveals that long shaggy hair was in style for boys back then. Scanning class pictures, you see row after row of smiling faces, all sporting an almost identical hairstyle—parted in the middle, long bangs, over the ears on the sides, and just past the collar in the back.

That's the way almost every guy wore his hair in the seventies—well, every guy except Randy.

While his parents, good loving folks, gave Randy a fair amount of freedom in some areas of his life, they allowed him no leeway when it came to his hair. While his classmates relished their rock star locks, Randy, once a month, was sent to the barbershop for a GI Joe cut. Being a compliant, obedient, firstborn, Randy did as he was told.

But oh, how he *hated* having hair that was so different from everyone else's.

This is best illustrated by an experience he had one day as he was eating lunch in the cafeteria. A girl he sort of knew—a popular and pretty member of the school newspaper staff—came up to him and asked if he would mind posing for a picture to illustrate a feature story she was preparing for the paper.

Well, sure! Randy was flattered. What was the picture for? Basketball? He had, after all, played really well during last night's game. No? Maybe for National Honor Society? Stage Band?

Well, no. None of those. The pretty girl giggled. She was writing a feature story about *old-fashioned* things verses *modern* things. Randy—more accurately, Randy's hair—would be the perfect illustration she needed for *old-fashioned* things.

What time tomorrow could he pose?

The next day, Randy, who had never ever in his entire life lied about being too sick to go to school, did just that. When his dad came to wake him up, he coughed, sniffled, and feigned nausea. If it had been necessary, he would have played dead. In Randy's mind, *anything* would have been better than having his picture in the paper because of his short hair.

What's the Big Deal?

I've often mused that of all the challenges parents of adolescents face, the greatest is to not make mountains out of molehills. We can all recall times when our parents, like Randy's, stood firm on an issue when it might have been more appropriate for them to bend. Figuring out which issues are mountains and which are molehills can be difficult. When it comes to our sons' personal appearances, on what matters should we take a stand, and on what issues should we be more tolerant?

Parents hold a variety of ideas and beliefs about acceptable dress. What is thought to be appropriate for specific situations varies from one part of the country to another. It even varies from one community to another. In our home we've utilized the following basic rules about dress and grooming:

1. Your look must be appropriate for the occasion.

2. You must appear modest and decent.

We've found that the fewer specific rules we make, the better. Styles and situations change. These two basic guidelines will cover almost every situation.

We must stand firm on such issues as health, safety, and morality. Clothing is not one of those issues. Wise parents will allow their sons a great deal of freedom to dress as they please. Boys can safely express their individuality through their appearance.

Sometimes they will choose styles that we hate. Sometimes they'll wear items that make their grandfather think that something is wrong with our parenting skills. *What were we thinking letting him out of the house like that?* If a son is into extreme styles, rule number one will come into play often. What's appropriate for wearing when he's hanging out with his friends will not be acceptable for family reunions and church. On the other hand, if his choice of clothing complies with both of the rules, it's time to back off. Just because we don't like it doesn't mean that it's not all right to wear.

It's a Fact

"I wasn't doing anything wrong. How come that guy asked me to leave?"

Twelve-year-old spiked-hair Jake, dressed in jeans three sizes too big, a black T-shirt with the sleeves ripped off, and knee-high, lace-up boots, expressed genuine surprise and indignation at being asked to leave his favorite music store at the mall. Jake was a good kid, tall for his age, a leader in his church youth group, a Boy Scout, and a member of the academic honor society at his school. The "tough guy" look was a new one for him, one his parents had reluctantly allowed him to try.

"Think it might have something to do with the way you were dressed?" asked his mom. "Maybe the clerk was afraid you were going to shoplift or cause some other kind of trouble."

"That's not fair. Just because I look a certain way doesn't mean I'm a bad person. It's just fashion. I like the way these clothes feel."

"You're right," Jake's mom replied. "It's not fair. People shouldn't be judged by how they look. *But they are.* It's a fact. If you choose to look a certain way, you can expect to be treated a certain way. Next time you go to the mall, maybe you'll want to tone it down a bit. Maybe not. Whatever you decide, realize there are consequences."

Jake's mom's message is a helpful one. One our sons need to be taught. Freedom in any area of life, even in how we look, brings with it increased responsibilities and consequences. Folks who don't know us react to us based on what they see.

Especially at the mall.

Permanent Alterations

It's not a big deal when guys like Jake try on a variety of looks. They can wear one set of clothes today and try something else tomorrow. If they bleach their bangs, the blond will grow out. Long hair can be cut, shaved heads will eventually have hair again, and striped socks can be traded in for plain white. Clothes and hair styles can be easily changed.

Not so with piercing and tattoos.

While parents can, without fear of lasting consequences, allow their sons lots of leeway when it comes to how they look, everything changes when the topic of discussion is a permanent alteration. No adolescent boy is ready to make decisions regarding changes in his appearance that will be with him forever. This is an area where there is no room for compromise.

If, when he is an adult, a son decides to pierce his eyebrows and tattoo his earlobes, well…(gulp) fine. That will be his choice to make.

But not until then.

End of discussion.

Blue Hair?

The first time I spotted 16-year-old Jerry sitting near the front of the church, I believed he was going for a patriotic look. Sporting red, white, and yes, *blue* spiked hair, adorned with numerous chains around his neck and both arms—chains that looked heavy enough to pull a stuck pickup out of a ditch—as well as an impressive array of scary-looking tattoos, he was impossible to miss. My husband and I were visiting a new church, one he and I and our daughter, Rachel, were considering joining. Our Russell had already moved out of state to attend college.

"Look. Do you see that guy?" I leaned over and whispered to Randy.

"Must be a visitor," he replied.

Of course. While looks like his wouldn't raise many eyebrows on a big city street, in the rural, small-town area of the Bible Belt where we were living at the time, his spiked hair and chains made for an unusual, scary look. Of course, if he, like Randy surmised, was somebody's cousin visiting from out of town—well, that explained it.

We talked about Jerry on the way home. "Rachel, did you meet the guy with the hair?" I asked.

"Uh-huh," she said. "His name's Jerry. Monday night's teen devo's gonna be at his aunt's house. Can I go?"

"Jerry's a member of this church?" asked Randy.

"Uh-huh," said Rachel. "Can I go?"

We visited again on Wednesday night. Jerry was standing outside the building when we drove up. He was wearing a black T-shirt with big, bright white letters that said *Got Crabs?* Never mind that he'd purchased the shirt at a popular seafood restaurant—one that specialized in steamed crabs. What was he thinking? I thought that the shirt bordered on obscene.

"How's the youth group?" we asked Rachel after class.

"Good. The kids seem nice."

"What about that Jerry kid?"

"I like him. He's really sweet."

Randy and I exchanged looks. *Right.* Maybe we better visit a while longer before deciding to join this church.

Turns out Jerry *was* a sweet kid. He was a kid who had a troubled home life, who had experienced much rejection. He and his behavior were far from perfect, but he loved

Jesus and toted a Bible wherever he went. Working with the teens at the new church, I grew to like Jerry, even love him, and to understand his overwhelming need to stand out. Jerry's outlandish looks were his way of getting the attention of adults. I believe they were also a test.

You say you love me, but do you really? Will you love me even if I dye my hair green? Purple? How about if I pierce my tongue? Will you love me then?

To the credit of the members of that church, they did love him. They loved him enough to overlook his outlandish looks, to accept him exactly the way he was.

As for Jerry, as he grew and matured in the faith, he was able to share the love of Jesus with a group of teens at his school who never could have been touched by the kids who looked more like they belonged in church.

Occasionally, as if to throw us adults a bone, he would dye his hair black or brown. In response, in the church foyer, we would gush over him, telling him how very nice he looked. Why, we hardly knew him, he was so handsome with his hair like that!

Jerry's response?

He would smile at us, say thank you, shrug, and show up the next week with his hair green.

While I'm still not fond of Jerry's wild and crazy looks, no longer do I see them as such a big deal. I'm glad that my son never went that far, glad that I was never forced to put my foot down to stop him from looking like that. We never faced the issues of tattoos or piercings, and orange was as bad as his hair ever got.

Bottom line? Jerry's a good kid. He is loved by the church, loved by the Father, and loved by me. Because of him, when I meet adolescent guys on the street whose looks give me pause, I see them in a different light.

Thanks Jerry.

For being such a good kid.

But just one thing. Would you do me a favor? Don't wear that black T-shirt to church.

Ever.

Got it?

Good.

> *The LORD does not look at the things man looks at.*
> *Man looks at the outward appearance,*
> *but the LORD looks at the heart."*

—1 SAMUEL 16:7

Lookin' Good!

1. Ask your son about the different groups at his school—the jocks, the preps, the punks, and the cowboys. What kinds of clothes do the different groups wear? Who decides? What would happen if someone in a particular group decided to dress in a different way?

2. Dig out your old high school yearbook. Look at it with your son. Show him students wearing popular styles. Share a laugh with him.

3. When he's having trouble fixing his hair the way he wants, offer to help. Purchase new hair products for him to try.

4. When he wants to dye his hair, help him with it. The results will likely be less disastrous, and you will have more input as to the shade that he chooses. If it turns out looking good, you will have scored a bunch of parental points.

5. If he tries out a new look and the results are truly awful, help him fix it. Avoid saying, "I told you so."

5
Hittin' the Books

Russell, a university student by now, is an intelligent guy. A champion on his high school's winning quiz bowl team, Russell has a great memory. Anything he hears or reads, he is likely to remember. His natural ability to recall information has, since Russell started school, made test-taking a breeze. He generally makes excellent grades on exams.

However, despite his great memory, Russell's semester grades usually fall in the "average" range. The reason? While smart, and good at taking tests, Russell possesses a sweet, calm, laid-back (a wee bit *lazy*) personality. Too bad for Russell that listening in class and taking tests is not all there is to getting an education. If that were so, he'd have had a shot at being valedictorian of his class.

For Russell and kids like him, academics take a turn south around the time they enter middle school. It's then that teachers begin to assign long-term projects and papers. Russell found it difficult to get motivated to do such things.

My friend Jeanna is an organized mom, one who's artistic and crafty and who loves to build and create. She was visiting from out of town when seventh-grader Russell decided to begin working on a major project that had been assigned five weeks before. It was due the next day.

"Mom," asked Russell, "have we got any boards?" It was past eight o'clock.

"I don't know. What do you need a board for?" I asked.

"Uh, my science project. I gotta make a telegraph machine."

Jeanna, whose kids were still very young, overheard. "That sounds interesting, Russell. How are you going to make it?"

Not very well, was my thought. Weeks ago, I had offered to shop if Russell would give me a list of items he needed for the project. He had declined, assuring me that he had plenty of time before it was due. There was no need to worry about it just yet, he had assured me. Knowing he needed to get the project done on his own, I had mentioned shopping for materials only a couple more times.

Okay, maybe half a dozen more times.

On this, the eve of the project's due date, Russell was finally beginning to sweat. The assignment, one-fourth of his final grade, involved the creation of a sturdy base, an overhanging arm, and a dangling instrument of some sort. I could have likely purchased the materials Russell needed to make the assigned contraption for around ten dollars at the local hardware store, which closed at five.

"Guess you'll have to use stuff we've already got," I said from my cozy spot on the couch.

"Maybe there's a board in the garage," Russell said with great hope in his voice. "Mom, do we have a saw?"

"Sure. In the tool box. I think it's in the trunk of Dad's car." Randy was gone in the car and would *stay* gone overnight.

"Oh."

It's hard to watch one's child suffer. At least a little bit hard. I stayed on the couch and with a withering look at Jeanna, convinced her to stay on the couch too.

It took several hours, but Russell finally went to bed, having completed what has to be the worst science project in the history of our school. Held together with hot glue instead of nails, crochet yarn instead of string, a pencil instead of a dowel rod, and with a base two feet too long, Russell's telegraph machine was quite a sight to behold.

Jeanna, who had envisioned a wonderfully designed, creatively engineered, painted, sanded, and labeled project was appalled. "Annette! You can't let him turn that in! He'll get an F!"

Jeanna was wrong. He got a D.

As for me? I was right to let Russell do it on his own even though it was hard to let it happen and harder still to watch him suffer the consequences of the bad grade. How do I know I was right? Jeanna told me so. These days, she's parenting a darling, easy-going, red-haired son named Ben—a sweetie who reminds me of Russell at that age. Ben, in seventh grade, was recently assigned a two-month-long project on the regions of Texas.

Need I say more?

Light a Fire

Many adolescent boys, like Russell and Ben, go about life unconcerned with things like projects and good grades. While lovable and dear, these guys can drive parents crazy. We want them to learn to rely on themselves and to have discipline and self-motivation, and yet we don't want them to fail a grade either! To motivate and guide these boys is a challenge. For many of them, the loss of privileges such as participation in sports is effective. For others boys, a parent could take away everything from the VCR to the use of indoor plumbing. Neither restriction will bother them much.

While boys in early adolescence still need help with homework and such, now is the time for Mom and Dad to *begin* to back off. It's appropriate for us to provide our sons with the school supplies they need, to praise them when they work hard on their school work, and to follow through on agreed-upon consequences should they not do their best. Limiting TV and computer time and making sure that he's getting enough sleep will help a boy's academic efforts. However, as our sons move towards maturity and independence, our goal should be for them to be ultimately responsible for their own school performances.

Early adolescence is the time to start shifting accountability for schoolwork from your shoulders to his. By the time a boy is in his last couple of years of high school, the total responsibility for getting his work done should be his. After all, few of us plan to attend college with our sons! The time to begin making preparations for their academic independence is now.

Public Sinners

Upon the successful completion of his first week of kindergarten at our neighborhood public school, Russell's granddad took him out for his favorite McDonald's lunch. "So, Russ, do you like school?" asked Granddad.

"Yes."

"Is your teacher nice?"

"Yes."

"Have you made some friends?"

"Yes."

"What's your favorite thing about school?"

"Well, Granddad, I really like—" Mid-sentence, Russell took a big gulp of Coke.

"Excuse me?" For the life of Granddad, it sounded exactly like Russell had said "sinners." Surely not. He must have misunderstood. Granddad waited till Russell had finished his slurp, then asked him to repeat his favorite thing. "What's that again, buddy?"

"Sinners." Russell let out a big burp. "S'cuse me."

Lands! *Sinners* was exactly what the little guy had said. Granddad had heard on A.M. radio that public schools weren't what they used to be, that they had gone *liberal,* but this beat all. "Son," he said with concern, "tell me about these sinners that they have up at your school. What kind are they?"

"Well you see, Granddad," said Russell munching on a Happy Meal fry, "there's an art sinner and a music sinner, a block sinner where they have blocks, and a book sinner where they keep all the books. I really like the kitchen sinner even though all of the food is fake. Me and my friend Ryan like the sandbox sinner the best. Granddad, can we get ice cream?"

Whew. Granddad gave Russell a big grin. "Sure, son, you can have ice cream. I'll go get us some. You want it in a cone?" *Centers.* Of course! Public education hadn't gone to the dogs after all.

School's Where It's At

Most families, like ours, choose to utilize local public schools for their children's education. While our sons' and daughter's academic experiences have been far from perfect, public school has worked out fine for us. Since our children's births, we've lived in small communities where traditional, rural values are still held dear. The majority of our children's teachers have been Christians. Many of them we count among our personal friends.

Such is not the case in other areas of the nation or even in every school district of our chosen home state. Some families discover that their local public schools are unacceptable for a variety of reasons. They find that they become even more unacceptable as their sons reach the adolescent years. Drugs, gangs, fighting, immoral or anti-Christian courses of study, and low academic standards plague some of our nation's public middle schools and high schools.

Private schools, even Christian schools, are not immune to problems. Some of them provide wonderful, nurturing educational environments; others do a terrible job. Many excellent schools take downward turns when the administration or staff changes.

If ever there is a time parents need to be actively involved in the content of their children's education, the adolescence years are it. Parents need to be aware of what is being taught at school, but more importantly, they should know the school's climate of discipline and level of overall order. Astute parents can, with lots of discussion and instruction at home, correct a certain amount of teaching material that goes against core family beliefs—material such as evolution taught in science class or discussions about the normalcy of homosexuality taught in health class. However, no amount of talking at home can counteract eight or more hours a day spent in a truly toxic situation.

If a son feels continually threatened, if he is learning by the example of the majority of his classmates to be disrespectful of authority, or if he is overwhelmed by constant noise, chaos, and disruption, it's our responsibility as parents to intervene on his behalf.

Think of it this way. When we adults find ourselves in intolerable working conditions at our jobs, we have options. We can request a transfer to another department, talk to someone in the personnel department, or even quit our job and find another. Students don't have those same choices. Yet at some time in their educational careers, many boys find themselves in school situations that are truly unbearable. Perhaps they are being bullied day after day, or even made fun of by a cruel teacher. It could be that no matter what they wear or how they comb their hair, they face daily teasing because of the way they look.

How would we adults feel if every morning we arrived at our jobs with the expectation that we would face the same kinds of treatment—or worse—from our coworkers or boss? How would we feel if we believed that we had *no recourse* but to deal with the situation as best we could for four, five, or even six years? We should not expect our children to deal with situations that we, as intelligent, grown-up adults would find intolerable. Just as we have breaking points and sometimes *must* escape, so it is for our children.

If there is a problem at school, a boy may try to hide it. He may rightfully fear retaliation should his parents take action and become involved. It's still our job to protect and nurture him. As moms and dads we must know our sons and be familiar with the behaviors they exhibit when they're under stress. If they're reticent to talk, we need to ask them questions. If we suspect a problem, we need to talk to teachers, administrators, and other parents.

Being aware of problems that exist at school is not always enough. We must love our sons enough to prayerfully take action should the situation be one that is dangerous to their physical, mental, emotional, or spiritual well-being. Our boys should understand that without a doubt, we care. We, their parents, are on their side. No situation is without hope.

Bottom line? Our sons must have the assurance that we will see to it they're safe and will always get the help or the relief that they need.

Resolutions

If we think it best that we keep our son in his current school setting, then depending on the problem, a move to another class, to a different teacher, or to another campus may be the answer. Sometimes a simple, seemingly small change is all that's needed. However, should such a move not be enough—should a son's current school situation be truly unbearable and unresolvable—parents need to be willing to instigate drastic change, even if it's costly or inconvenient.

A son may need to move from a public school to a private school, or from one private school to a different one. Even though a school has the word "Christian" in its name, it may not be right for your son. Look carefully at the overall learning environment at the school before making a decision to enroll your son.

Homeschool is the choice for a growing number of families. Thousands and thousands of parents have made the decision to devote time and attention to educating their children themselves. It may be daunting to think about beginning homeschool late in a son's academic career, but many families have done it successfully. The decision to homeschool doesn't have to be forever, though some parents and children enjoy it so much they can't imagine ever going back to away-from-home school.

If a son needs to be taken out of public or private school, if bringing him home seems to be the very best thing—go ahead. Give it a try. Other homeschool families are the best resources to help you get started. Could be that in a year or two, he and you will be ready to go back. Then again, maybe not.

Not Everything's Such a Big Deal

Thankfully, most problems at school are not terribly serious. They are irritations and misunderstandings that do not endanger our sons in any way. Minor problems usually can and should be handled by our boys themselves. A boy gains confidence when he resolves a problem on his own. Only if a son flounders in his attempts to resolve a situation should we step in and request a parent-teacher or parent-administrator conference.

Parents who intervene every time something doesn't go their son's way rob him of the opportunity to grow and mature in his ability to tolerate situations that are less than ideal. He also needs to learn how to effectively resolve conflicts with his peers and with those in positions of authority. If a son is not facing serious threats to his body, his mind, his emotions, or his spirit, give him the chance to work things out on his own.

Perhaps a son is whining about not getting as much playing time during basketball games as he thinks he deserves. Encourage him to have a respectful talk with the coach. If he chooses not to do so, let him live with the playing time he is getting. Should he bring home a test that he believes his teacher graded incorrectly, suggest that he either accept the grade or stay after school to discuss the matter with his teacher.

We would *love* to step in and help our sons out. For some of us, it is against our very natures to do *nothing*. But these situations and others like them are opportunities for us to encourage and empower rather than rescue. It's our job to teach our sons how to handle conflicts and problems.

Education Is Forever

The purpose of school, whether in a public facility, a private setting, or at the kitchen table at home, is twofold. In order to live as productive adults, our sons need to know important basics like reading, writing, science, history, and math. More importantly, our boys need to be impressed with the fact that education is valuable and that learning is a process that takes place for a productive, mature person's entire life.

A son may not...okay, probably *won't* glean that lesson on his own, but parents can teach this principle by modeling lifelong learning at home. Tell your son about training you receive at work. Share with him how things in your business change all the time, and how you must learn new things in order for you to effectively do your job. Explain to him why you read news magazines and *National Geographic* as well as *Sports Illustrated*. When you are striving to learn something new, such as computer programs, woodworking, bread baking, or conversational Spanish, share your progress with your son. When you're struggling with a concept or a new skill, voice your frustrations. Let him see that learning new stuff doesn't always come easily, but that even so, you don't give up.

School's Not So Bad After All

As I write this, Russell, the kid whose science telegraph machine project didn't look like much more than a giant rickety mouse trap, is midway through his junior year at college. While most of his friends have changed majors two, three, some of them even four or more times, Russell has not wavered in what he wants to do when he graduates. It seems he won't be leaving school for...well, ever. He wants to be a coach and a history teacher.

"So, Russell," I ask. "When you graduate and get a teaching job and you've got a room full of American history students, are you going to make them do projects and papers and stuff?"

"No way," he says. "Never. Lecture Monday through Wednesday, review sheet on Thursday, test on Friday."

His dad and I look over at each other and grin.

We'll see.

Of making many books there is no end,
and much study wearies the body.

—ECCLESIASTES 12:12

Learning's Great!

1. On every gift occasion, along with toys, clothes, or games, be sure to give your son at least one book. Adolescent boys prefer books with lots of action and activity. They also enjoy biographies. If he's not a great reader, search out books that, though on a lower reading level, will capture his interest.

2. Look for a class you and your son can take together. Community colleges are great places to find low-cost courses like woodworking, karate, or foreign language. Don't be surprised if he learns some things more quickly than you!

3. If you live near a college or university, befriend a residential student. Invite him to share a weeknight meal with your family, or to watch a Sunday afternoon football game on television. Ask him about his courses, about what he plans to do, and about what he enjoys about campus life.

6
Don't Kiss Me in Front of My Friends

Volunteering to host Thanksgiving for our extended family means a commitment to house and feed a huge, noisy crowd. There's a bunch of us, and our ranks keep increasing. Over the years, older members of the family have passed to glory, but we keep adding new spouses, children, and close-as-kin friends. Every year, on Wednesday night before the big day, family members begin their descent. On through Thursday noon they trickle in: grandparents, aunts, uncles, and cousins, as well some folks we count as family members even though we're not sure *what* to call them. It's a great time.

The year Russell was twelve years old, we planned to host the holiday gathering at our house. In preparation, I scrubbed, polished, and shined the house. I stocked the fridge with goodies for the feast and did as much ahead-of-time cooking as I possibly could.

It was important that everything be just right.

I counted chairs and napkins and gathered matching plates, figuring out as I went just exactly who would sit where. Thankfully, we had a dining table that, with the addition of three leaves, was long enough to seat all the adults—if we scrunched up just a bit. As for the children, I would put them in the family room at card tables. When I counted up all of the folks who I knew would be coming, my seating arrangements came out just right. Should unexpected stragglers show up, there were several folding TV trays in reserve.

Thanksgiving morning, I crawled out of bed before dawn to put the turkey in to roast. By 10 A.M., the house had filled with yummy smells: praline-topped sweet potatoes, corn-bread dressing, and pumpkin pie. My kitchen was jammed with so many helpful female relatives that there was hardly room to work. Outside, cousins and young uncles played football in the sunshine.

As far as I could see, everything was perfect.

At least it seemed so until after the prayer. Once the "Amen" was said, everyone moved to take their suggested seats. That's when the trouble began. Russell—remember, twelve years old—feigning nonchalance, purposefully plopped himself down at the big table—the one I had set for the adults.

"Uh, Russell," I said, "you're in the living room. The adults are going to sit in here."

"This is where I want to sit."

"Sorry, bud. Not enough room. Hop up. Take your plate into the family room with the rest of the kids. I've got tables all set up."

"Uh-uh. I don't want to sit with the kids. I'm going to eat in here." Russell's jaw was set in a way I'd not ever seen. What was this? Public back talk from my compliant, nonconfrontational son—the child whose good manners drew compliments from strangers?

"It's okay," said Russell's favorite uncle. "I'll eat with the kids."

"No, it's *not* okay," I interrupted. No son of mine was going to behave in a disrespectful way towards a guest. This stubborn display was so unlike him! What in the world was he thinking—expecting one of the adult relatives to move just so that he could sit where he wanted. Not wanting to create a bigger scene than we already had, I leaned down and hissed in his ear. "Russell. Up. You and I are going into the bedroom for a little talk."

Sympathetic—towards Russell, that is—relatives averted their eyes. Seething but defeated, Russell scooted his chair back and stood up.

"We'll be right back. Y'all go ahead and have a seat," I said as we headed towards our private talk.

I won that day. The seating arrangement, that is. Russell sat with the kids. I sat with the adults. But I also lost. I embarrassed my son, as well as my guests. He, at twelve, was feeling like a man. And no wonder. Like the men, Russell had helped haul heavy loads of firewood in from outside. He had been included in his uncles' domino games—he'd even been a coveted partner. When his grand-dad had gone to the corner store for ice, he had gone along. Unbeknownst to me, Granddad had let him drive the quarter mile back. After a great morning spent feeling like one of the guys, being relegated to the kid table was a parental slap on the face. Worse, my public reprimand had humiliated him.

I didn't understand then, but older and wiser, I do now. The situation that took place on that Thanksgiving ten years ago wasn't about bad manners.

At least not my son's.

Standing Tall

Russell's behavior at age twelve was predictable and normal. My misguided attempt to make him behave in what I perceived to be a mannerly way came across as a put-down. He was saying, "I'm growing up. I don't feel like a little kid. I feel like an adult."

My response to him, though unintentional, was both flippant and disrespectful. It came across like this: "A man? What are you talking about! Why, you're just a child."

Boys this age are stretching towards manhood and independence. In a few short years they will be there! In the meantime, they tell us by their actions and their words that they don't feel like little kids anymore. They don't want to be treated like little kids anymore either.

See if you recognize any of the following behaviors in your son. These are some common ways boys express the feeling that they feel bigger, stronger, more grown-up.

- He used to be affectionate in public, unashamed of goodbye kisses in the car outside his school. Now he's hugging the door, and he's out and on the sidewalk almost before you stop the car.

- He's never able to finish his meal, but he balks at ordering from the kids' menu. At ten years old, he'll qualify for the discount meal a good two more years.

- He checks every few weeks to see if maybe, just maybe, he is now taller than his mother.

- When he wrestles on the floor with his dad, there's a new intensity. It's hard to tell he's playing. He tries to pin his dad, longs to make him be the one to cry uncle.

- There are grimy fingerprints above one of the inside doors of your house. Every time your son walks through it, he jumps straight up in an attempt to touch the door frame, the wall above the frame, and finally the ceiling.

Boys this age are terribly sensitive to being treated like children—even though they still act like children much of the time! Their bodies are growing and changing. Fueled by surges of testosterone, they feel more manly. To be told "you're too young" or "you're too little to do that" is to be insulted in the worst way. They feel grown, and they wonder why their parents don't understand.

The Boy Will Have Milk

Recently, I witnessed an adolescent drama at a local restaurant. Seated in a booth across from my friend and me were three men, each a generation apart. Their facial resemblance caught my eye. Their conversation, close enough for me to hear, caught my ear. Grandpa, well-dressed in pressed slacks and a starched white shirt, sat on one side of the booth by himself. Dad, balding, with a slight belly paunch, sat across from him on the outside. Son, about 14, tall with big feet, hunched shoulders, a bad haircut, and a moderate case of acne, was seated against the wall, next to his dad.

Soon after they were settled, a cute young waitress came to take their beverage orders. Ignoring both Grandpa and Dad, she flirted, just a bit, with the son.

"Haven't I seen you somewhere?"

He smiled and blushed. "I dunno."

"You look familiar. Do you go to college here?"

"No, but I might some day." He sat up a bit straighter.

"You ought to. It's a good school. Do you play sports?"

"Basketball," his voice cracked.

"We've got a great team. Maybe you could come to a game sometime."

Thirsty, Grandpa cleared his throat. "I think we're ready to order."

She took the hint, but winked at the son. "Great! What will you gentlemen have?"

"I'll have iced tea," said Grandpa.

"Coke for me," said Dad.

"I'll have—"

But before his son could get the words out of his mouth, Dad interrupted. "The boy'll have milk. He can't have carbonation. You know, because of those bumps on his face. Doctor says sodas might make 'em worse. Right, son?"

If the son could have squeezed under the table, he would have, so deep was his embarrassment and shame.

"Have those right out for you," she said. "Anything else?"

A hole to crawl into for the son, best I could tell.

Parents Goof Too

I've no doubt. That man loved his son. His granddad loved him too. It was obvious that both of the older men enjoyed being with the teen. He appeared well cared for. There's no doubt that the boy's dad was concerned about his son's health—or at least his complexion! Yet with his thoughtless words, the dad momentarily crushed his son's confidence and self-esteem. In my mind, I can still see the stricken look on the boy's face. I recall how, for the rest of the meal, every time the cute waitress came by, he stared at his plate.

Most of us have said or done things just as bad as what that dad did in the restaurant. Unfortunately, no parents get it right 100 percent of the time. The transition of boys into men takes place at such a ragged, unpredictable pace, it's no wonder we mess up. It's difficult to remember that the skinny guy who watches Saturday morning cartoons and sleeps with a light on is the same young man whose voice is changing and who suddenly likes girls.

Words that embarrass or hurt can't be taken back, but they can be apologized for. When we say or do something disrespectful or inappropriate to our son, when we embarrass him, we need to tell him we're sorry, we made a bad mistake, and we'll try our best not to do it again.

Silence on the Home Front

Lots of preadolescent boys are nonstop chatterers. They love to be in the middle of everything. In the kitchen, they talk about school, their friends, and their teachers. On the way home, they tell us everything that happened during Sunday school and their Cub Scout meeting. These are the boys who can take an hour and a half to recount the plot of a 30-minute sitcom. They are often underfoot, and they sometimes talk so much that our ears get sore. "Will he ever be quiet?" we wonder. "Will he ever learn to entertain himself?"

Oh, yes. If he's like the majority of adolescents, he'll be quieter than we would prefer. We won't see as much of him as we would like. Many adolescent boys become reluctant to talk—at least to their parents. They feel a need to pull away, to be separate. It's normal for adolescents—even friendly, social ones—when asked about how their day has gone, to respond, "Okay," and leave it at that. Boys this age are feeling the need for increased privacy. They begin spending time in their rooms with the door closed.

When this shift towards clamming up instead of spilling out occurs, when a boy shows us by his words (or lack of them) and by his deeds that he needs more space, that he desires to put some distance between himself and us, we need to respectfully give it to him. This process is normal and healthy. None of us are as close to our parents or as dependent upon them today as we were when we were children. So it's with our sons. Though his pulling away may hurt our feelings or make us feel a bit melancholy, it's a sign that our boys are maturing, growing, and developing exactly as God designed.

When a boy begins to show signs of greater independence, many parents err in one of two ways.

Too Much Space

A common mistake parents make is to pull back too far, to give a boy too much autonomy and freedom. If you have a son who is unusually mature for his age, one who is basically responsible and compliant, it's easy to relax, to back off from him, and to assume he is fine. If he's prickly and moody, it's tempting to assume that the best course of action is to leave him alone. I see many well-meaning parents who lack involvement in their sons' lives. They feel their boys neither need them nor want them as much as they did when they were younger. The fact that sons begin this separation process during the same years that their parents' careers, church, and community commitments become more demanding makes it even easier to slip up in this way.

Honestly? Communicating and keeping up on what's going on with a secretive, noncommunicative adolescent is hard work. Some of us are just tired!

If you've lost touch with what's going on with your son, it's never too late to improve. Begin by orchestrating time together when there's little else to do but talk. Repetitious, outdoor chores such as painting or weed pulling, done together, are conducive to conversation, as are long trips together in the car. When alone with your son, ask him questions that cannot be answered with one syllable.

For every boy, there are conversation triggers that will spark his interest. Here's a sampling of effective conversation starters gleaned from parents who have told me they worked for them. Almost any son will be moved to talk about one or more of these hot topics.

- Your sister has asked me to take her to her friend's house. She says there'll be boys there. Do you think she's too young to go? Should I tell her no or okay? What do you think?

- Someone told me the government is considering moving the age a person can get their driver's license to 18 because young drivers cause most car accidents. Do you think that's a good idea?

- Lots of schools are requiring students to wear uniforms. How will you feel if your school decides to go that way? If you were part of the committee deciding, what kind of uniforms would you choose?

- Girls say they should be allowed to join the Boy Scouts. Do you think that's a good idea? Why?

Close, Just Not *That* Close

While some parents back off from their boys so much that they lose touch, other parents unwittingly thwart their sons' moves toward independence and autonomy by being *overly* involved in their lives. These are usually the energetic parents who enjoyed wonderful teen years themselves. They can't wait until their boys begin to participate in the adolescent activities that were so much fun for them so they can be a part of things again. They love chaperoning field trips, being the Team Mom, and hosting parties and church youth group events at their house.

If you are one of these parents, great! Just use a bit of restraint. Boys love involved parents—to a point. Boys don't need or want their parents to be so involved in every activity that they never have the opportunity to participate without them. Sons need to learn how to behave at someone else's house, how to cope on an out-of-town youth trip without Mom and Dad. They need the chance to occasionally try out their social skills without parents watching and listening.

Some parents—and I, embarrassed, confess to this one—pry details from their sons that they have no need or right to know. *Who was there? Is Kay still going out with Jason? Who sat with who? What did you do first? What next? Then what did he say?* For some reason, I just love to hear all the juicy details. If you're a mom, I'm betting you do too.

Yet, when we grill our kids in such a way, when we insist they tell us *everything,* we rob them. Adolescents have their own culture, their own language, their own codes of conduct that are designed to be exclusive of adults— parents in particular. They have that right. I'm convinced all kids have secret lives. I'm *not* talking about issues of health, safety, or morality, such as drug use or sex. Parents should use every method possible to keep abreast of a kid's involvement in such, being as intrusive as the situation dictates. What I *am* referring to is the normal private stuff kids talk about among themselves. The same things that, when we were 12 or 13, we discussed for hours with our best friends but never with our dads.

I can always tell when I've crossed the line and pushed too hard for information that's none of my business. My kids clam up. They become secretive and evasive. Especially after I've manipulated them into telling me details they didn't intend to, they will zip their lips.

And I can't blame them!

He's Growing Up

The task of the adolescent is to grow, mature, and become a unique person, separate from his parents. We can help him to do so with grace and good humor, or we can make it difficult for him. Either way, it's going to happen. Wise is the parent who celebrates the signs of a son's independence.

And blessed is that parent's son.

> *When I was a child, I spake as a child,*
> *I understood as a child,*
> *I thought as a child;*
> *but when I became a man,*
> *I put away childish things.*
>
> —1 CORINTHIANS 13:11 (KJV)

Steppin' Out on His Own

1. If a son shrugs off hugs and dodges kisses, respect his right to do so. Punches in the arm, tickle fights, and knuckle rubs to the head are poor substitutes for big bear squeezes, but most parents find that they'll do in a pinch!

2. If your son's neither talking nor listening, write him a note. One day, leave a letter of affirmation for him on the bathroom sink. Another day, list three things he does that make you proud. Let him be surprised to find the list under his pillow.

3. When your son expresses a need for more freedom, counter his request with the offer of increased responsibility. Explain to him that the two will increase at the same rate. He wants to pick out all his own clothes? Great! Now's also a good time for him to begin doing some of his own laundry. He believes he's too old to be told when to go to bed? Fine. Purchase an alarm clock for him so that he can get up and ready for school without promptings from Mom or Dad. In this way, he gets the freedom he desires, and you are teaching him life skills and responsibilities he needs to know. Both of you win.

7
Just One of the Guys

I remember Russell's first birthday. Perched in his high chair, he celebrated with a frosted chocolate cupcake washed down with cold milk from a sippy cup. Having just moved, Russell, his dad, and I were living together in a married-student housing complex on the university campus to which we had just moved.

While the colonial-style house we live in today is not a large one by any standard, the entire apartment we lived in back then would easily fit into our present living room. Sharing that little complex with other young student families was an experience in near-communal living. We got to know our neighbors really well. Because the apartments were so small, few things were kept secret. When our Asian neighbors prepared dinner with something called fish sauce, we knew. When a husband got locked out of an apartment because his wife was mad at him, we knew. When, after some sweet talk, she decided to let him in, we knew. And when they decided to make up—well, if they happened to live in one of the apartments on either side of us, we knew that too.

It was while living in that university town that we met our friends Gwen and Tommy. They had just gotten married. Even though Tommy was still in school, he and Gwen were eager to start a family. They played with Russell, asked us questions about what it was like to be parents, and dreamed of when they would have a baby of their own.

It didn't take them long.

That November, Gwen gave birth to their first son, Caleb. Randy and I were so happy for them. A little boy—now their family was just like ours.

"Guess what! Gwen and Tommy have a little boy like you," we told Russell, who by now was almost two. "His name is Caleb, and he's going to be your new friend."

"Can I see he?" asked Russell.

"Not today, not tomorrow, but the next day you can," Randy promised.

The day that Tommy brought Gwen and baby Caleb home I had a two-dozen-balloon bouquet delivered to their door. *To Caleb from Your Friend Russell,* the card said.

Tucked away in a family photo album is a picture of Russell sitting stiff legged next to Gwen on the couch. He's got a big sweet grin on his face. In his lap he's holding his new best friend, three-day-old Caleb.

Caleb's too big for Russell to hold now. Both of the boys took after their dads. Tommy is at least a head taller than Randy. Caleb, a basketball player and over six feet tall, towers over Russell. It's been more than 18 years since the boys first met. Today, at ages 19 and 21, they are still good friends. Last summer Caleb was employed by the Christian youth camp where Russell has worked for the past three years. This fall, Caleb became a freshman at the same out-of-state university where Russell is a junior.

Lifelong friends? Russell and Caleb are among the few guys I know to whom that phrase truly applies. When Gwen and I see them together today, no longer our sweet little guys, but now deep-voiced, hair-faced young men, we can't help but sigh and remember the day they met.

While from-birth relationships are rare, the long-term friendship Russell and Caleb share is not. Likely your son has a special companion who's been a part of his life for a long while too. Friendships will shape our boys' futures. The relationships your son forms today will, in part, mold him into the man he will become.

Friends till the End

Who among us can forget the looks of adoration bestowed upon us by our boys when they were little? They sat on our laps, looked deeply into our eyes, and told us we were the best mommies and daddies in the whole world. They gave us sticky kisses and colored homemade birthday cards for us. When we came home from work, they instantly dropped whatever they were doing to race into our arms, sometimes nearly knocking us over in their enthusiasm.

Those were the days weren't they?

If you've got an adolescent boy in your house, it's likely that kind of unbridled admiration and hero worship has, shall we say, *waned* just a little bit?

Boys this age crave less time with their parents and more hours with their friends. They listen less to their moms and dads and give greater attention to the opinions of their peers. They shrug off words of parental advice in favor of wisdom gleaned from 11- and 12-year-olds. So great is the pull of a boy to his peer group, it's no wonder many parents lament what they perceive to be the end of their days of influence.

Thankfully, that's not really so. Despite the inevitable, normal, and healthy shift towards greater involvement with friends that occurs as sons reach adolescence, we, as concerned, loving, and involved parents, continue to have the greatest impact of anyone on our sons. Our influence is bigger than that of teachers, media, and yes, even friends.

Fitting In with the Group

Boys long for the acceptance of their peers. Like puppies, they need to feel like they're part of a pack. Which pack? A positive one, we parents hope, for the group with which our son decides to identify will have a great impact on his behavior. His choice of friends will affect the way he dresses, his speech, the music he plays, the way he decorates his room, and even the way that he walks.

Doubt this? Park outside a middle school around the time school lets out for the day. Observe the students. What do you see? How many distinct "looks" can you count? In my part of the country a few of the groups easily observed are the "jocks," the "preps," the "punks," the "cowboys," and the "goths." Unsure about the definition of one or more of these groups? Ask your son. If he's an adolescent, he knows, and he can tell you lots of interesting details about them.

Guiding Him

Being a part of a group is not a bad thing. We adults like to fit in too. At work, at church, and in the neighborhood, there are groups of folks to whom we gravitate simply because we enjoy their company or feel comfortable in their presence. The challenge is to guide our boys toward good groups and away from less-desirable peers, and to empower them to stand up for themselves and their values when the group goes against what they have been taught at home.

Not an easy task.

Talk to your son about friendships and the need to fit in. Let him know you understand how important it is for him to have a group of friends to hang out with. Ask him about the different groups at his school. How are they different? Which ones get along and which ones don't? Do some groups get into more trouble than others? Do some groups look tough when really they aren't? Do teachers act suspicious of some groups and accepting of others? Why is that?

When talking about his friends and the groups at school, try to do so calmly and without placing judgment. Avoid making assumptions based on what you've heard. Sometimes what parents hear through the grapevine is nothing more than gossip. Recently, in a nearby small town, a new-to-the-community 13-year-old was labeled a drug user and thug because he wore black jeans instead of blue ones and had red eyes as a result of chronic allergies. When the rumors got back to his mother, she was understandably distraught. Her son did not use drugs, and he had never been in any trouble with the law. Who knows how such hurtful rumors get started? When dealing with the reputations of kids, we parents should have our facts straight.

When there's a need to warn your son about certain boys or instruct him that he must avoid certain groups, do so by talking about specific behaviors you do not approve of. Lower your voice and speak gently, so you don't slip into the parental "attack" mode we moms and dads are so famous for. The idea is to convey information and instruction without putting our sons in the position of defending a person or group.

Getting to Know the Guys

Parents need to know their sons' friends. And the best way to know them is to maintain an open house. Tell your son his friends are welcome to come over *anytime*. Try to always say yes to his requests to have friends spend the night. Many of us do not relish the idea of our houses having revolving doors. We like things to be tidy. Just last month we made the final payment on our light beige couch! We enjoy order and quiet. At the end of a stressful day, a house full of noisy kids does not sound fun.

Won't a bunch of rambunctious boys make a mess of our house? Absolutely. Will they eat up a week's worth of snacks in one night? Yep. You can count on it. Not only that, your son's friends will spill soda on the sofa and make a mess in the bathroom. They will forget to refill the ice trays and neglect to turn off the lights when finally, after you've told them three times, they do go to bed. You may have managed to teach your son to put the toilet seat down when he's finished, but his friends will leave it up every time.

So—is all this worth it? Do you wonder about the payback for all the time, trouble, and expense involved in turning your beloved home into what is essentially a free restaurant and hotel for the next several years?

The reward is twofold. First, if your house is appealing to your son and his friends, that means that he'll be spending more time at home where you can keep an eye on him, and less time out and about—a situation which prompts even the best of us worry. Having kids underfoot—both your own and others'—makes for fewer sleepless nights! Second, maintaining a welcoming home, one that values kids over carpet, opens the door for you to know your son's friends and for them to know you. A boy who has eaten a meal at your house is less likely to try and talk your son into doing something that he knows goes against your family values. By listening to and observing the guys who hang out at your house, you'll achieve a depth of knowledge about local teen life you couldn't obtain any other way.

When guys arrive, be friendly and welcoming but give them space too. Though adolescent boys can be lots of fun, they neither need nor want parents around who act like they're just part of the gang. There's no need to disappear to the other room when kids are over—in fact drifting in and out to keep an eye on things is a really good idea—but don't make yourself a constant presence in the middle of their fun.

Show genuine interest in your son's friends. If you watched them play well in last week's basketball tournament, compliment them. When their picture is in the local paper because of some award, save the clipping for them. Ask about their new pet. If you like it, comment on a new shirt that they're wearing. Boys love the attention of friendly adults.

Bad Boys

Perhaps you are like me. I have friends who bring out my best. After spending a couple of hours in their presence, I come home refreshed and inspired, in a positive frame of mind, ready to be a better wife, mom, and friend. Do you know anyone who affects you like that?

There are also people in my life who almost always bring me down. When I meet them for lunch, I find myself, despite my best intentions, gossiping, saying negative things about my husband, and whining about how things in life just aren't going the way they should. When I've spent time with these folks, I can count on a rotten mood for the rest of the day.

Can you relate?

If we adults are influenced by negative peers, how much more so are our sons? This comes as no surprise. From the time they were toddlers we've observed our boys, following an afternoon spent with certain friends, coming home and acting in out-of-character ways—running around and being rude, unusually aggressive, hyperactive, or silly.

Nothing changes in adolescence except that the stakes get much higher.

An adolescent boy will behave like the friends he chooses to identify with. If a son is acting out, abusing drugs, drinking, smoking, or skipping school, you can be almost 100 percent certain he has a negative peer group.

If a son is repeatedly involved in behaviors such as fighting, destroying property, or staying out late without permission; if he has a sudden drop in grades or becomes disrespectful of all authority; he may need to be completely removed from his current group of friends. Accomplishing this seems like an almost impossible task. Yet a son's very life may be in danger.

No boy is perfect. They all make mistakes. Not every active kid who gets into a little trouble is a troubled kid. But some of our sons are troubled. Even boys who have enjoyed carefree, happy childhoods sometimes hit a skid during adolescence—often as a result of negative peer influence. If you see a change in your son's behavior—not just a few isolated incidences of poor judgment, but an entire shift in his demeanor—be aware. Don't ignore danger signs, expecting him to grow out of it. If you suspect a serious problem with your son, seek wise council. Talk to his teachers, to school administrators, or to someone at your church. Take him to a Christian counselor or psychologist for testing.

Be prepared to separate your son from his peer group if that's what he needs. This discussion is about boys age 11 to 14. It's both possible and entirely appropriate for parents of boys between these ages to monitor and forbid contact with negative peers. When a boy is in his mid to late teens, parents will not be able to exert such control.

If separation from peers is the course you take, know that your son will need your help to make new friends. He may need to be moved to a different school or to be home-schooled. Though a drastic measure, there are times when a family needs to move to a different town so that a child can get a fresh start.

Parenting means putting our children's needs before our own. In serious situations, the cost of doing so may be great.

The rewards will be priceless.

Friends Indeed

Some boys are by nature friendly, talkative, and social. Ten minutes in a room with a group of guys and they feel right at home. Friendships come easily to them. Because they forge bonds so naturally, these boys don't give relationships much thought.

Other boys are quieter by nature. They may be shy, or they may simply feel uncomfortable around people they don't know well. Making new friends, while not impossible, is difficult for them. Rather than laying claim to a bunch of running buddies, they're more likely to be loyal to a handful of close friends with whom they share the same interests.

Two different types of boys. Two different styles of relating to their peers. Both perfectly normal—and neither in need of a parent's help. If we have a gregarious personality, but have been blessed with a quieter, less outgoing boy, many of us feel the need to fix him. Problem is, he doesn't *need* fixing! He's happy the way he is.

Sometimes a son appears to have *no* friends. Unfortunately, some boys manage to always say or do the very things that alienate or anger their peers. A boy with no friends is a lonely kid. If you see your son struggling in this way, intervene on his behalf. Seek out a counselor skilled in caring for adolescents. There's effective help available for boys who need help making friends.

Healthy friendships enrich our sons' lives. Some of our boys' friendships will last for life. Others will wither after a short season. All are valuable for what they bring to our sons' lives. Nurture them. Encourage them. Stand back and enjoy.

Good Old Joe

When Russell was in the seventh grade, we broke sad news to him. Because of Randy's job, our family would be moving to a town three hours away where he had no friends. So distraught was even-tempered Russell that he lay down on the carpet at our feet, clutching his head and groaning as if our words were causing him physical pain.

"You'll be okay. You will," we told him. "Listen, Russell. It's not like you won't make *new* friends. It won't be so bad."

But for many months it *was* so bad. Settled into our new town, enrolled in his new school, Russell was terribly unhappy and lonely. Every day, he would come home, drop his books, grab a snack, and plop down in front of the television.

He would not want to talk about his day. Any of it.

But I would. Every afternoon, out of my mouth would pop the same series of questions. "Did you make a friend today?"

"No."

"Did you talk to anyone today?"

"Not really. But I did say excuse me when I sneezed."

"Did you sit with anyone at lunch?"

"No, Mom. I didn't."

"You ate your lunch all alone?" My baby. Had to eat his lunch alone. Is there anything worse for a mother than the picture of her child eating his school lunch all alone? I wanted to cry, and sometimes I did—though not when anyone was looking.

After a couple of weeks of this routine, Russell's answer to my incessant questions changed. "Yes, Mom," he announced proudly one Friday. "I made a friend today."

"You *did!* Russell, that's wonderful! What's his name?"

"Uh—Joe."

"Joe? He sounds nice."

"I guess he is, but he gets in trouble a lot."

"He does?" My eyes narrowed. "What kind of trouble?"

"All kinds. Nothing really bad. Joe's a good guy."

And so began a new after-school routine for Russell and me. Every day he would come home with something new to tell me about Joe.

Joe had seven sisters. *Seven?*

Joe didn't play football. At his last school he'd been on the water polo team. *Water polo? Hadn't Joe last lived in a town in the Appalachian Mountains?*

Joe got in trouble in computer class for sneaking into the lab early and changing all the screen savers into running advertisements for Joe's Dating Service.

Joe dyed his hair blue for a day and wore seven fake earrings in one ear. (Since Joe got queasy just trimming his toenails, real piercings were, sadly, out of the question.)

So outrageous would be Russell's tales of Joe's playful misbehavior at school, some days I'd nearly fall out of my chair laughing. Russell would laugh too. Best of all, Russell ate lunch with Joe every day. He told me so.

It was only when I called his hand, when I finally insisted that he bring Joe home to meet me, that I learned the shocking truth: *There was no Joe.* My good-natured son, desperate to escape my questions, eager to make *me* feel better, had invented someone to have lunch with, someone he knew I'd like.

I did like Joe. I wasn't ready to give him up.

So I didn't.

For several more weeks, Russell kept me up to date on his friend's latest shameless shenanigans. It was not until a few days before Christmas—by then some *real* friends had crept into our afternoon conversations—that I realized Joe was no longer around. We hadn't spoken of him in a very long time.

And while Russell's flesh and blood friends are nice enough, I admit it. Sometimes I miss Joe.

He was, after all, Russell's (and my!) first new friend.

Two are better than one, because they have
a good return for their work: If one falls down,
his friend can help him up. But pity the man who falls
and has no one to help him up! Also, if two lie down together,
they will keep warm. But how can one keep warm alone?
Though one may be overpowered, two can defend themselves.
A cord of three strands is not quickly broken.

—ECCLESIASTES 4:9-12

Pals Around

1. Speak well of your friends to your son. Let him see how you help your friends, how you look out for them, and how you forgive them when they make you mad. Your example shows him how he should treat his buddies.

2. Plan an outing with a friend and his or her son. Do something the four of you, either mother and sons, or fathers and sons, can enjoy together, such as attending a sporting event, going on a hike, or visiting a local farm or ranch.

3. Host an end-of-school bash for your son and his friends. Encourage him to invite all the guys in his class—even those who are not his best friends. Serve hot dogs and cookies or build-your-own sub sandwiches.

4. When one of your son's friends is ill or is having problems at school or at home, mention him by name during family prayers.

8
Look, Mom—
No Hands!

This past December, while he was at home from the university during Christmas vacation, Russell and I went out to lunch together. His twenty-first birthday was only a few days away, and I was feeling a bit introspective. "Hard to believe you're almost a legal adult," I said. "Seems like only a little while ago you were marching into kindergarten with your new Mickey Mouse lunch box. A year from now you'll be doing your student teaching and getting ready to graduate."

"Uh-huh." Unmoved by my sentimental musings, Russell chewed his steak.

"You know I'm proud of you, don't you?"

"Yeah, Mom. I know."

"You've been so easy. You never rebelled or gave your dad or me cause to worry."

Russell gave me a wicked grin. "There's still time."

I let *that* remark slide. "Seriously. True confession: When you were younger, did you ever sneak around to do something bad? Something that Dad and I still don't know about?"

"Sure. Lots of things."

"You did?" I set down my fork. "Lots? Like what?"

"Remember when I was 13 and you and Dad would go out to eat or to the movies sometimes? You'd make me stay at home and baby-sit Rachel."

"Sure. I remember. You were very responsible. We wouldn't be gone for more than a couple of hours. We'd order pizza for you two and tell you to stay inside the house until we got back. You always seemed to like it when we left you alone. There were never any problems that I remember. Were there?"

"Not really. But we didn't exactly stay in the house."

"No? Where'd you go? Next door?"

"Nope. Joe Bob's. You remember—the store down the street."

Down the street nothing. Joe Bob's was a good three blocks away.

"You'd walk to Joe Bob's? And take Rachel with you?"

"Yeah. We'd wait till we were sure you and Dad were gone. We'd hunt around the house for some change to buy some candy or a soda with, and then we'd take off."

"Russell! I can't believe it." I'd had no idea. "You'd take your sister that far when you weren't even supposed to go outside? What I can't believe is that Rachel never told."

"I always told her that I'd buy her a treat, but only if she promised not to tell."

"You sneak!" I said. "But why Joe Bob's? There were snacks in the house."

"I know. I just wanted to see if I could do something I wasn't supposed to and not get caught."

"Which obviously you did!"

"Well, once you and Dad forgot something and came back home to get it. Five more minutes and you would've met me and Rachel walking down the street. That was close!"

From the faraway grin on his face, I could see that the memory of those risky, forbidden hikes to the store still gave Russell pleasure.

Risky Business

If it's tall, they'll climb to the top and leap off of it. If it's moving toward them, they'll try to outrun it. If it looks too unstable to hold them, they'll jump up and down on it. The fact is, most boys are *driven* to take risks. When asked, they can't explain why they do the crazy, illogical things they do. It's just fun! They crave the feelings of being invincible and powerful.

Dads understand these drives to do foolish and dangerous things better than moms do. Matter of fact, most dads will, with the slightest of promptings, recount stories of their own off-the-wall adolescent antics.

There's absolutely nothing wrong with boys being boys—aggressive, active, and fearless. God made them that way. The challenge is for parents to ensure that their boys stay safe. When our sons were toddlers, a trip to the emergency room could fix a split lip—the result of a tumble off the back of the couch or out of a tree. If our little boys tried to swim in an area over their heads before they knew how, we were right beside them, plucking them out of the water and drying them off. As long as we watched them really closely, we were usually able to keep our little guys out of danger. Other than a few scrapes, maybe even some scars, the risky behaviors of little boys usually inflict no lasting harm.

That's not so any more.

When boys reach adolescence, because of their increasing independence and autonomy—no longer are they under our watchful care every minute of their days—their inborn drives to take risks can lead them into dangerous situations. The enticement of some risky behaviors, especially the use of tobacco, alcohol, or illegal drugs, can exact a great cost on their lives.

Everybody's *Not* Doing It

A neighbor once told me that she believed all teenagers will eventually try alcohol and probably illegal drugs too. In her mind, such "experimentation" was a normal part of growing up—one that parents had little control over.

I don't buy her way of thinking. The truth is, most boys will not become involved in any type of substance abuse. The majority of adolescents don't smoke or drink alcohol. Yet while we expect the best of our boys, astute parenting lessens the chances that our sons will become involved in destructive behaviors. We are not powerless. Our influence on our sons is great. Parents need to be educated and aware of the temptations their boys face and able to recognize the signs that they may be in trouble.

Up in Smoke

With all of the education, all of the public service ads, and the myriad of warnings kids hear left and right, one would think that no boy would ever be tempted to smoke. And the truth is, fewer of them are starting. Figures from the National Household Survey on Drug Abuse show that the number of new teen smokers fell by one-third between the years 1997 and 1999. That's the good news. The bad news is that according to The National Institute of Drug Abuse, 12.2 percent of eighth graders surveyed in the year 2001 reported smoking cigarettes within the past month.

That's a lot of kids. *Eighth grade.* Sounds young, doesn't it? But according to *Growing Up Drug Free: A Parent's Guide to Prevention,* children face the greatest risk of starting to smoke in the sixth and seventh grades. Even younger children, those in the earliest elementary grades, are commonly introduced to cigarettes by older siblings or friends.

To Drink or Not to Drink

No adult I know believes tobacco use is, in any way, okay. Even those who smoke don't defend it, for they realize it's addicting and harmful to their bodies. Most smokers wish they'd never started. Many make frequent attempts to quit.

However, lots of responsible, grown-up folks are less clear when it comes to the use of alcohol. Is it wrong? Sinful? Can a Christian drink moderately? Could drinking be okay for me but not okay for you?

There are convincing cases to be made for both sides of this hot issue. I know faithful Christians who have studied, prayed, and sought godly counsel only to arrive at opposing positions. So what's a parent to do? Many moms and dads, unclear about their own views about alcohol consumption, end up conveying fuzzy values about drinking to their boys. Unfortunately, adolescents don't *do* fuzzy! With boys this age there are no gray areas. Issues are either black or white. They need clear-cut instruction about what is right and what is wrong.

How can parents take a stand against drinking when they believe that maybe for some people it's really not wrong?

Easy.

Drinking is never, ever okay for kids. End of discussion. In my state, Texas, and in most others, it's illegal for anyone under the age of 21 to consume alcohol. Not only is it unsafe and unhealthy for kids to drink, it's against the law.

Randy and I taught Russell our personal views about drinking. During his growing-up years he heard sermons about drinking and about drunkenness. The use of alcohol was the topic of discussion many times in his church youth group. On the campus of the Christian university he attends, students caught using alcohol may be dismissed.

The approach that Randy and I have taken is this: Underage drinking is always wrong. We forbid it. If either of our children were caught drinking underage, they would be punished. Once they are of legal drinking age, the choice to drink or not to drink is theirs. Maybe their adult views will be the same as ours. Maybe not. But until then, they have no choice.

Evidence on His Face

For more than a decade, I've spent a week or two each year in Mexico serving with medical evangelistic teams. We usually travel to rural areas where, because of poverty, even basic health care is out of the reach of most of the population. Because we go to such remote areas, generally we see more burros than buses, more cornfields than cars.

Not so on a trip I made last winter. We spent much of the week serving in a large Mexican city. Each day, I rode with other team members on city buses from the house where we were staying to the area where our mobile medical and dental clinics were set up.

A ride on a crowded city bus in Mexico is quite an experience. Depending on the driver's taste, riders are treated to music ranging from salsa bands to Selena to Celine Dion. Those who get lucky have seats, but the majority of the folks stand jammed together in the aisles, holding on during frequent stops, easing aside when other riders need to get off. I'm a people watcher, and I enjoyed observing the young mothers with their children, the men going to work, the old couples who helped each other along. I also had a great time studying the teenagers. In many ways they weren't much different from the teens back home. Trendy clothing and crazy haircuts are the look of choice for teens on both sides of the border.

On one late-afternoon bus ride toward the end of the week, a boy about 11 or 12 years old caught my eye. I was seated, but he stood in the aisle directly in front of me. Dressed in raggedy jeans, coming-apart sneakers, and a thin T-shirt, he had done something odd to his eyebrows and to the front of his hair. It looked like he had applied some kind of silver dye. *Kids!* I thought. *The crazy things they do.* I watched him for a bit. Then it hit me. The substance in the boy's hair was not an adolescent attempt to adorn. It was silver spray paint, the result of a recent episode of paint sniffing—"huffing," as the kids call it.

My stomach turned over and my heart broke. From the size of the boy, I would guess that he still had his baby teeth. Because of my work with troubled kids, I knew that every episode of inhalant abuse causes a degree of brain damage. If any kid anywhere needed every bit of brain power he had, it would be a poor boy living in Mexico.

For the rest of my ride, try as I might, I could not take my eyes off the boy. Our lives were worlds apart. There was nothing I could do except remain in my seat and pray for him. And as I sit here in my home office on this day, I can recall exactly what it felt like to sit on that crowded bus. At this moment, in my mind, I can see the boy's face.

And so, once again, for him I pray.

Kids and Drugs

Children who use drugs often start around the ages of 12 and 13. Generally they begin with the illicit use of legal substances—tobacco, alcohol, and inhalants (paint, glue, and other household products). Sometimes, though not always, they progress from those substances to the use of illegal drugs; marijuana is usually the first. As a young marijuana user gets older, he often abuses other drugs.

While smoking and drinking often precede the use of various other drugs, they don't *cause* their use. It's just that drug users generally begin with less lethal, more readily available substances. Few kids who have never smoked a cigarette or taken a drink of alcohol will be inclined to use crack cocaine.

Don't Ignore the Signs

Some common signs of alcohol or drug use include:

- poor grades in school, especially if he has previously been a high-achieving student

- skipping school

- withdrawing from the family

- appearing depressed

- tired all the time, sleeping more than usual

- aggressive, rebellious behavior

- decline in caring about personal appearance

- change in friends

- increase or decrease in appetite

- decline in general health, including weight loss, runny nose, red eyes, frequent infections

- money missing

What to Do?

Isolated incidents of smoking or drinking alcohol may be just that—one time occurrences. They should be met with much discussion, appropriate punishment, increased restrictions, and stepped-up parental vigilance. I am of the conviction that no matter how old a boy is, no matter where he has gone or who he has gone with, parents should wait up until he arrives home. A goodnight kiss and hug is a great time to sniff a boy's breath. Insisting upon a verbal accounting of how the evening went is an excellent way to assess his mental state.

But should an incident of substance abuse happen more than once, should you note signs that your son has a tobacco, alcohol, or drug problem, don't go it alone. Seek professional help immediately. Get referrals from your family doctor, from the counselor at your son's school, from the minister at your church. If the first person or facility you consult does not appear to be right for your son, try another one. Keep trying until you get help for your son. Appropriate professional intervention early on can determine the future of your family and of his life.

Protecting Our Boys

So much discussion about substance abuse may make you feel uncomfortable, anxious, and fearful about what lies ahead as your boys reach adolescence. Don't let it! Again, most boys will *not* get involved in drugs. Most will *not* choose to smoke or abuse alcohol.

If your son has smoked cigarettes or drunk alcohol, you can usually stop his behavior by handling the situation carefully. There are no perfect kids. Good boys make big-time mistakes. If your son makes an error in judgment, don't give up hope. Be swift, be firm, and watch his behavior more closely than you've ever watched before, but let him know you love him, you believe in him, and you will never write him off or give up on him—no matter what.

Prevention Starts at Home

There is much parents can do to safeguard sons against the use of tobacco, alcohol, and drugs. Try this: Ask any adolescent (not your own) who in his life has the most influence on him.

The media, would you guess?

Friends?

Teachers?

None of those. Over and over you will hear from boys themselves that their parents are the most important influence in their lives. By staying involved in our sons' lives, by teaching them clear, consistent values, we can do much to prevent them from becoming involved in substance abuse.

Simple things like having dinner together (without the TV), supporting a son's involvement in extracurricular activities, assigning and following up on chores, monitoring his television viewing and the music he listens to, and imposing a curfew decrease a boy's chances of involvement in substance abuse. And boys growing up in families who worship together regularly are much less likely to smoke, drink, or use drugs.

Expect the Best

From the time they were born, we parents have done our best to keep our boys safe—even when it seemed that their goal in life was to make yet one more trip to the emergency room! We worry about these risk-taking sons. We warn them. We threaten them. We pray for them. But most of all, we love them and trust them to a heavenly Father who loves and cares for them even more than we do.

A prudent man sees danger and takes refuge,
but the simple keep going and suffer for it.

—PROVERBS 22:3

To receive the booklet *Growing Up Drug Free: A Parent's Guide to Prevention* free of charge, call the Department of Education's toll free number, 1-800-624-0100 (in the Washington, D.C. area, call 732-3627), or send your name and address to Growing Up Drug Free, Pueblo, CO 81009.

Also available is *Keeping Your Kids Drug Free: A How-to Guide for Parents and Care Givers.* This resource may be obtained by calling 1-800-788-2800 and requesting document # PHD 884, or by going to the Web site www.health.org.

Tough Talk

1. Share news reports of drunk driving accidents with your son, especially those involving teenagers. Talk about how choices teenagers make can affect their lives and the lives of their friends.

2. Role play. Ask your son to pretend that the two of you are at a party. You be the "bad" kid who tries to influence him to drink. Ham it up. Be as "bad" as you can be!

3. When watching professional sports on TV, talk to your son about the beer commercials you see. Point out how commercials only show drinkers having fun. Ask him if he thinks the ads are realistic. If not, why not?

9

God and Me

That Sunday night was one that 14-year-old Bryan, the son of my friends Kevin and Julie, will always remember. After the evening worship service, Bryan, along with the rest of the youth group, sauntered over to the fellowship hall for what he expected would be the usual end-of-school chili dog supper and devotional. Instead, when Bryan walked in, he was stunned by the nine-foot banner proclaiming, "We'll Miss You, Bryan!" draped across the back wall of the fellowship hall. He was overwhelmed by the stack of going-away gifts placed at his feet, and embarrassed by the tears that clouded his eyes when, at the evening's end, his church's youth leader led 60 teens in prayer for him and his family.

It was quite a send-off.

Seven days, 200 miles, and a mountain of packing boxes later, Bryan and his parents joined their new church family in worship for the first time. When they walked in, Bryan's first thought was that this was the smallest church building he had ever been inside.

His second thought was that *everything* looked really old. The carpet was old, the hymnals were old, and even the preacher and most of the members looked ancient.

From where he sat on the back pew, Bryan counted two teenage guys, a girl that was probably in junior high, and three babies. That was it. Obviously, he would enjoy no more Sunday night snack suppers, no teen devotionals, and no father-son church workdays.

Bryan wondered if there would be anything at all for him in the church of less than 80 members. And though they didn't express their doubts to anyone but each other, Kevin and Julie wondered the same thing. The situation did not look good. The town to which they had moved was tiny. When Kevin and Julie asked around, they learned that none of the local churches offered much in the way of special programs for teens.

Kevin and Julie cared deeply about Bryan's spiritual development. Had this move been a terrible mistake? How could Bryan possibly grow in faith without an active church youth group?

A Spiritual Life of Their Own

When it comes to nurturing and rearing our boys, the most critical task we parents face, the one thing we do that matters the most, is to successfully guide them toward personal relationships with God the Father. Nothing else we teach our sons will ever compare with the importance of impressing upon them the eternal significance of God's truth in their lives.

And for many boys, these are the years when their tender hearts are more open to those truths than at any other time in their lives. For not only is adolescence a period of rapid physical growth, development, and change, it's also a time when boys mature spiritually—sometimes by leaps and bounds. Because of their growing intellects and increasing abilities to grasp more abstract concepts, boys this age are able to understand more of the Bible, to ask intelligent questions, and to truly seek God's will for their lives.

It's during these adolescent years that many boys move from obediently but blindly accepting the faith and religious observances of their parents toward making their own deep and personal commitments to God. At this point in their lives they have the ability to grasp a greater understanding and a more meaningful acceptance of Jesus Christ as their risen Savior. Some of them, for the first time ever, feel a need for God's mercy. Many times, with great relief, they stake a claim on God's grace for their lives.

These spiritual steps toward maturity are giant ones and thrilling for us parents to observe. Over the years, I've spent time with lots of adolescents—not only my own, but those who belong to other proud parents as well. Over and over I have been amazed and humbled at their spiritual hunger and at the depths of their repentance. The passion that they display when confronted with the love and mercy of Jesus takes my breath away every time I see it.

Home's Where It's At

While lively, spiritually directed youth programs are beneficial to adolescent boys, the greatest predictor of faithfulness in kids is surprisingly neither the size of nor their participation in a church youth group. Rather it's the spiritual atmosphere at home. Youth group activities only supplement the influence of the home, for it's what goes on there that will, to a great extent, produce faithful sons who become faithful men. While exceptions can be seen everywhere, most often, God-directed parents will have God-directed kids.

Is that news not enough to make all of us parents feel uncomfortable? You bet it is! None of us are perfect when it comes to our walk with God. We mess up with disheartening regularity. It can be discouraging to realize that we, flawed and unworthy, wield such influence and power over our sons' spiritual development.

Yet here's the great news.

We don't have to live sinless lives to be good examples to our boys. What we must do, however, is be honest. Adolescents can forgive many things. What they can't tolerate are adults who pretend to be perfect when they're not. So, when the situation we've gotten ourselves into is one that's appropriate to share, we parents need to acknowledge to our boys that we've messed up. If our sons hear us use foul language, they also should hear our words of repentance and how we're trying to honor God with our lips. If we have a problem with gossip or misplaced priorities, we can share those struggles too. In order to experience grace in their own lives, boys need to see us accept the forgiveness of a loving God when we sin.

It's from what they see of their parents' relationships with God that boys will pattern their own approach to Him. Most of us pray, read the Bible, and meditate on spiritual things. Yet do our boys know that we do? Do they see us sitting quietly with an open Bible in our lap? They need to.

One of my husband's most vivid memories of his grandfather is this: Every time Randy went to visit, he would see his granddad's Bible lying open on the arm of the couch, but never open at the same place.

Get into the habit of discussing with your son what part of the Word you are currently reading. Share with him how you are praying for the needs of a coworker. Ask him to pray too.

Examples speak loudly, but some spiritual truths will be learned only if we speak of them out loud to our boys.

When we talk of spiritual things and our sons act uninterested, bored, or even embarrassed, we who are committed to rearing boys with strong faiths just keep on talking!

Church Is Not a Choice

Belonging to a church and meeting regularly with a body of believers strengthens us, our families, and especially our sons. For our boys to see that regular attendance is important, church needs to be more than just a place where our family shows up on Sundays. It should be a body to which our family belongs, one which is dependent upon us just as we are dependent upon it. Our family's relationship to a church family should be such that our presence there makes a difference in the lives of other members.

When sons grow up and move away from our homes, it becomes their decision whether or not they will be a part of a church body. Adolescent boys are not ready to be given that option.

We see to it that our sons go to school. We make sure that they take their vitamins, do their homework, floss, and visit the doctor and the dentist regularly. About such matters, we don't give our boys a choice. Similarly, parents are responsible to ensure that their sons go to church. Families are strengthened by worshiping and serving together. Seeking out a church family that works for Mom, Dad, and the kids, where everyone feels wanted and needed, creates an added bond of family unity that's often missing when kids go to one church and their parents go to another. The leadership of the church we choose to work and worship with should see its younger members as vital to the church of *today* and not wait for them to be the church of *tomorrow*.

Learning to Serve

I made my first week-long medical mission trip to Mexico when Russell was eight years old. Randy stayed at home and took care of Russell and his sister, Rachel. When I returned from my trip, I told the three of them about some of the things I had done and seen.

"Were there kids there?" Russell asked.

"Lots of kids."

"Were they sick?"

"Some. But not all. There were three boys just your age who played with a soccer ball in the yard across the street from where we had clinic."

"Next time, can I go with you to Mexico?" Russell asked. He'd heard me talk about other team members who had brought their older kids on the trip with them.

"I don't know about that. Maybe," I fudged. Truthfully, the trip I'd just returned from had proved extremely tiring. Team members had worked long hours and spent even longer hours traveling cooped up together in a crowded van that was not air-conditioned very well. I didn't think that at age eight, Russell was old enough to tolerate the trip. "Tell you what…perhaps you can go when you turn ten."

My thinking was that Russell would probably lose interest in going to Mexico.

No way. For the next two years, every time mission trips to Mexico were discussed at home, at church, or with family and friends, he piped up, "I get to go on a mission trip when I'm ten. Right, Mom? That's what you said. Remember?"

Each time he and his dad and his sister helped me load my bags to go on yet another trip, he'd remind me, "When I'm ten I'll get to go. Right, Mom?"

And so despite my fears that he might still be too young, the fall after Russell turned ten, he and I and the rest of our team loaded up our stuff, piled into a church-owned van, and headed toward the border.

You've never seen such a grin!

I'd talked to Russell off and on for months about how he was expected to behave on the trip. *Don't complain. Don't drink the water. Don't feed the dogs. Shake when someone offers you their hand. Be polite. Smile. Sit still during church.*

Russell did everything I told him to do and more. He was a trooper even though the treacherous mountain roads scared him so badly that he covered up his head with his jacket and cried really quietly so that no one would hear. He slept in an icy-cold room with two very large men who snored really loudly—but he didn't complain. I heard him gag only a little when, as guests at dinner one night in someone's home, we were served a Mexican stew that contained whole chicken feet—soft, yellow, yucky chicken feet that were every bit as awful as they sound!

It was obvious that Russell enjoyed himself that week. He spent much of his time playing with the kids who were waiting in line with their moms to see the doctor. He also helped pack and unpack supplies from the van every day. He moved benches and performed the tedious task of divvying up the large stock of bottles of aspirin and vitamins into tiny plastic bags.

On the way home, I looked over and saw Russell sleeping, slumped against the window of the van. *What had he gotten out of this trip?* I wondered. He had missed a couple of days of school. *Had it been worth it? Had seeing the poverty and the needs of the people, serving them in the ways that he had, affected him? Had he learned anything?*

I needn't have wondered. On the Sunday after we returned home, in preparation for Thanksgiving Day, his Sunday school teacher asked the class to make a list of some of the things they were thankful for. I would have expected Russell to name his Nintendo, the TV, or his Dallas Mavericks official team jersey. After all, he was ten years old.

But no. He named none of those things. When I sneaked a peek at Russell's list, here's what I saw:

1. clean water

2. medicine

3. heat

4. houses with real floors, not just dirt

5. ice

I miss Russell these days. Since he's away at school, his dad, his sister, and I don't get to see him very much. While he makes it home for a few days at Thanksgiving, for Christmas, and for a few weeks in the summer, he spends his spring break every year somewhere besides at home with us. For the past three years he's traveled to Mexico, to help with his church's annual mission trip.

Much as I would like to spend the week with my son, how can I complain?

Christian service—any helpful task done in the name of Christ—gives our sons true feelings of belonging and of being needed by the body of Christ. We need to see to it that our sons have opportunities to perform Christian service regularly. Doing so doesn't have to involve anything as major as a mission trip. Raking leaves for an elderly neighbor, writing a letter to a missionary, or even hanging around after Sunday morning worship services long enough to place hymn books back in the racks on the back of the pews are easy ways to incorporate the habit of service to others in your son's life. Give a boy a task, work beside him on that task, praise him for a job well-done, and watch his energy and enthusiasm soar.

Bryan's Gonna Be All Right

Shortly after the move, Bryan told Julie about his disappointment at not having a youth group in the new church.

She shared his feelings of loss. She told him that she missed her women's Bible class. Not many women in her age group were part of the new church. She agreed with him that she was not yet as comfortable in the new congregation as she was in their old one.

Julie did remind Bryan that the family had prayed for weeks about the move and that lots of people were praying for them still. She talked about God's steadfastness and His unchanging love for them, especially for Bryan.

Feeling especially grumpy one Wednesday night, Bryan confessed to his dad that Bible class was boring! His dad agreed that sometimes he, too, was bored by a sermon or distracted during a prayer. But he reminded Bryan that although worship and study are performed by imperfect, sometimes boring people, they are acts directed toward a magnificent, perfect God who is never boring.

Bryan went to church camp that summer for two weeks. His parents quietly helped pay for one of the teenage boys in the congregation to go with him. The two boys returned home good friends.

One Saturday morning, after enjoying pancakes cooked by Julie, Bryan and two other teens mowed, edged, and raked the yard of a member of the congregation who had

had surgery. Bryan's dad helped, but the teens did most of the work.

Bryan loved to sing. The deacon in charge of organizing the public worship services recognized his vocal talent. Within two months of moving to the new church, Bryan was asked to select and lead the songs for every worship service.

He was awkward and nervous at first, but he took the job seriously, selecting songs to fit with the preacher's sermon topic. Bryan's confidence soared under the love and appreciation of the members of the new church.

Two years have passed since Bryan and his family moved to their new home. Although Bryan has made lots of friends and likes his new school, he still misses the youth group from his old church.

His parents wish they could give him what he misses so much. However, they don't worry a lot about Bryan's spiritual development. Although children have their own free will and make their own decisions, Kevin and Julie believe that Bryan is going to be just fine.

So do I.

For you have been my hope,
O Sovereign LORD, my confidence since my youth.

—PSALM 71:5

Faith Boosters

1. Make sure your son has an age-appropriate version of the Bible. Lots of great student versions are available. Ask your pastor or youth minister to recommend one. Surprise your son with a cover for his Bible. A variety of masculine-looking, teen-worthy styles can be found at Christian bookstores.

2. Using sticky notes, post short verses of Scripture in prominent places in your home—on the fridge, over the computer, and above the kitchen sink. Be sure to replace the notes with new ones every week or two.

3. Tell your son you are praying for him. Ask him to pray for some specific need that you have, such as a problem at work or a health concern.

4. Speak respectfully of the leadership of your church. While it's appropriate for your son to realize that even folks in leadership make mistakes, he needs to hear you speak well of those who have been called to lead.

10
Roll 'Em

"Hi Mom," 11-year-old Sam greeted his mom, Dee, who is also my good friend. Home from school, he dropped his backpack on the floor and then shed his jacket, his shoes, and his sweaty athletic socks. They landed on the floor. "What's for snack?"

"Nothing—until you put your stuff away. After you do, peanut butter bars. And milk. How was your day? School go okay?" Dee got a knife out of the drawer to cut the gooey treat, made from scratch and still warm from the oven.

"School was good. I made 88 on my math test."

"Great!"

Sam disappeared into his room with his stuff. When he came back to the kitchen, Dee set his snack down at his usual place at the bar. She poured herself a diet soda and sat down with him.

"Mom, can I go see *Titanic?*" Sam asked, his mouth full.

"Nope."

"How come? I heard it's really, really good."

"*Titanic's* rated PG-13. That's why."

"That doesn't mean anything, Mom. Long as it's not rated R, I can get in. Only R-rated movies have bad stuff."

"Sorry. No can do," said Dee.

"My friends are going. Even Joey."

Joey's dad was a minister.

"My history teacher said that she thought it would be *educational.*"

"Has she seen it?"

"No, but…"

"Sam," Dee explained, "when you get older, maybe you can see certain PG-13 movies. But not until then. If the people who rate the movies think that it's not appropriate for you to see, you actually think Dad and I are going to say it's okay?"

Sam knew when he was beat. "No, I guess not."

"We'll do something fun this weekend. I promise," said Dee. "*Titanic*'s out, but maybe we'll go see something else."

Dee forgot about the conversation. Sam seemed to have forgotten it too.

Not so.

Two weeks later…"Where are you and Dad going?" Sam asked his mother, who he could tell was hunting for her keys.

"To the movies. Remember? I told you last night we were going. We'll be gone a couple of hours," said Dee.

"Whatcha gonna see?"

"*Titanic.*"

Sam's face went white. "Mom, you can't let Dad go see that!"

Dee looked quizzically at Sam.

He lowered his voice to a whisper. "Mom! You can't. There's a naked lady in that show! Joey told me." Sam, the one who had whined, "Everyone else is going—why can't I?" had suddenly appointed himself the family movie censor.

His mother suppressed a smile. "Oh, my. I didn't realize. Thanks for warning me, Sam."

"You're welcome, Mom. That was kind of close."

Dee agreed that it was. By then she had found her keys.
"Bye, Sam," said Dee as she and her husband left the house. "We'll be home by nine. Keep the door locked. If anyone calls don't tell them that you're home alone."

"I already know all that." Sam's parents said the same things every time that they left. Like he was going to forget or something. "Bye."

So. Was there really a naked lady in the movie *Titanic?*

Don't ask Dee. She doesn't know. Neither does her husband. Why?

Because they went to see something else!

Family Standards

The issue of what constitutes appropriate entertainment for adults is not the subject of this chapter. *Garbage in, garbage out,* is my personal belief. Yet people's ideas about what's okay vary widely. The lines of appropriate and inappropriate are sometimes blurry. Doubt it? Visit a big city art museum. Spend some time in the areas where paintings and sculptures of the great European masters are displayed. Anything there make you feel uncomfortable? Thought so!

Grown-ups are given the responsibility to decide for themselves what's moral or not moral, to choose what they will or will not view. Kids don't get those same choices. We parents are responsible for everything that our sons consume. Think of it this way: Most of us are mindful about the foods our kids put into their physical bodies. *Is this food product nutritious? Healthy? Is it not?* We worry about some foods being bad or even harmful to our boys' bodies. We don't allow certain things.

The same is true of the media our boys consume. Whether it be books, TV, movies, music, video games, or the computer, we parents, with just as much vigilance, need to monitor, limit, and even censor their media habits.

Boys and the Square Box

Think about the time your son spends watching television. Add up the number of hours every day that he spends glued to the set. Then, as best you can guess, total up the hours he spends watching every week.

Surprised at the number?

Most of us are. Many adolescents spend as much time watching television as they do in school. If our boys are spending this much time in front of the tube, we must face the fact that what they are viewing is having an impact on their development—physically, mentally, and spiritually. Is this much viewing time healthy? Does it benefit our sons?

Much of what's on TV is violent and immoral. That's reason enough to limit the hours spent watching. But suppose your son only watches wholesome, mostly educational programs. And suppose you only allow him to watch shows that you approve of, unless of course, he picks a video from your extensive G-rated collection.

Even so, there are still compelling reasons to limit the number of hours that he spends watching. The impact of too much TV viewing goes way beyond the influence of negative images and content. Our boys have only so many hours in their days. Every hour spent watching TV is an hour not spent on something more valuable and productive.

Kids who spend their time sitting in front of the TV are not outside doing other things. They become more sedentary, less active, and more prone to obesity. As the number of hours American kids spend watching TV goes up, the number of kids who are overweight also rises.

The hours a boy spends enthralled in a program are passive ones. While watching, he is being spoon-fed information. Not much thinking is required. It would be better for him to be doing some activity that would require him to engage his brain, to be creative and imaginative, or to solve a problem.

How can we parents limit our sons' TV time? What are some reasonable, doable ways to steer them to other activities?

Here are some suggestions:

Don't put a television in your son's room. Doing so encourages more viewing, not less, and it makes it *impossible* for you to monitor what your son sees. This no-TV-in-the-bedroom idea is not a popular one. Almost all of my friends have bought televisions for their children's rooms. TVs are popular Christmas gifts for kids. According to the Kaiser Family Foundation, 65 percent of America's children age eight and older have a bedroom TV. If your son already has a television in his room, think long and hard about the appropriateness of it being there. Being the parent, you can move it out, put it in the kitchen or family room, or even donate it to charity.

Limit your own viewing. It's hard for us to tell our boys not to watch too much television if we spend all of our free time watching our favorite shows. In some homes, if the TV isn't on, family members assume that the cable must be out! If that's true of your household, make a courageous change. Explain to your son that you have decided you've been watching too much and that you are trying to replace TV time with something better. Ask him to join you in taking a walk or playing a game. Though he may groan and complain, most boys, given the choice, will pick one-on-one time with parents over time with the TV.

Turn off inappropriate shows. Let's be honest. Even the offensive stuff that we see on television is sometimes hilariously funny! Some of the most intriguing dramas offered by the networks occasionally contain immoral situations or foul language. It's extremely tempting, especially as our boys get older and more sophisticated, for us parents to accept the unacceptable and to pretend that we are deaf and blind to what's taking place on the screen. When we do this, it gives our boys the message that we approve. Hard as it is, when bad stuff comes on, we've got to be willing to get out of the recliner and turn the thing off.

Even if the show is just getting good!

Cyber-Sitter

At ten-thirty last night, our daughter Rachel decided to download some information from the Internet about a couple of universities that she's considering attending when she graduates from high school next year. Which schools offered degrees in social work? Are they accredited?

I stood looking over her shoulder while she worked. *This is so cool,* I thought. *She found exactly what she was looking for in less than five minutes. Without the Internet, it would have taken us days to get this information by mail.*

And it is. Way cool. Yet home computers and the convenience of the World Wide Web have brought with them some real problems. Information is available 24/7. Good, helpful information. But the Internet also has a dark, dangerous side. Violent images, pornography, inappropriate chat rooms, sinister information, and sexual predators can be accessed by anyone who clicks a mouse.

Several months ago, when my husband, a high school teacher and coach, was interviewed for a new job, he was asked to name a few of his professional strengths and then to name some of his weaknesses. He explained that his strengths included being a team player, his abilities to teach kids in ways that match their learning styles, and knowing lots of ways to motivate and encourage. As for his weaknesses? Randy confessed that he was not good with technology. Lots of parents can relate. Those of us who did not grow up using computers like to joke about how our kids know more about their use than we do—that they are the ones teaching us!

If you've got an adolescent boy at home, it's likely that he *does* know more than you do about your home computer. That's okay. Utilize his expertise. However, what's *not* okay is having *no* knowledge about his use of the machine. If we choose to have a computer in our home, it's our responsibility to make sure that our children use it safely. If you are completely computer illiterate, take a class. Ask a friend to show you the ropes. Basic knowledge is essential to keeping your son safe. Here are some basic guidelines for safe computer use.

Computer Safety Tips for Parents

1. Locate the computer in the room where the family most often gathers, such as the living room or the family room. Position it so that the screen is visible to anyone who walks through the room. If your son has a computer in his room to use for homework, it should not have Internet access.

2. Be aware of what Internet sites your son is visiting. Your Internet service provider may provide blocking or screening services. Shop a large computer store for blocking software. If you are unsure how to install it, ask a friend to help.

3. Limit computer time. Even if he is not accessing harmful material, a son should not be spending hours and hours at a time sitting in front of the screen.

4. Pull up a chair. Spend time on-line with your son. Explore sites of common interest.

5. Set a good example. Technology can be isolating. Avoid spending hours on the computer that could be spent in family conversation or activities.

See No Evil

While exploring the Internet, boys may accidentally or intentionally see offensive material. Should you find that your son's viewing habits have been inappropriate, tell him what you have discovered. Explain to him why the material is not okay. Tell him that you understand his curiosity, but that viewing such material is not acceptable. If he has broken pre-set rules about use of the computer, a son should be disciplined. Restricting him from using the computer is usually the most appropriate action parents can take.

Of all aspects of computer and Internet use, chat rooms pose some of the most serious safety threats. Child predators can conceal their true identities and use chat rooms to make their first contacts with potential victims. Taking their time, they befriend young Internet users, gaining their trust and gleaning personal information. Many young boys have been exploited and hurt by such predators. Some have been killed. The dangers of spending unrestricted, unmonitored time in chat rooms cannot be overstated.

Many parents have come up with rules for Internet use. They discuss the rules and have their sons sign agreements to abide by them. Parents then post the list of agreed-upon rules directly above the computer. They review the rules frequently. Here's a sample of suggested rules. Adapt this list to your son's age and computer habits.

Parent–Son Internet Rules Agreement

1. I promise not to give out any personal information about me or my family. I will not give out my real name, my address, telephone number, or the name of my school without my parents' permission.

2. I will not send anyone any photos of me or my family without my parents' permission.

3. I will tell my parents immediately if anyone sends me any messages or information that make me feel uncomfortable, embarrassed, or afraid.

4. I will not agree to meet with anyone I get to know on-line unless my parents approve.

5. These rules apply to me every time I use a computer, whether I'm on my computer at home or using one at school, a friend's house, or the library.

Too Much Exposure

Sex sells. Adolescents buy. This fact has not been wasted on modern media. As never before, our sons are constantly exposed to overtly sexual material. Next time your son is out of the house, flip on the tube and watch a few minutes of MTV. When you pass a magazine rack, stop long enough to thumb through copies of a few of the most popular teen magazines. Tune in to whichever radio station in your area is most listened to by teens. Unless you are familiar with current teen culture, my guess is that you will be shocked by what you see and hear. Much of what influences adolescents in our culture is explicitly sexual in nature.

Even though *we* monitor what *our* sons watch, read, and listen to, they will grow up in this culture. They will be affected by it. False messages begin to sound true. These are some of the messages fed to our boys by some of today's secular youth culture.

1. Sex is always desirable, no matter what the circumstances.

2. Women are valuable only as sex objects.

3. Everyone is engaged in lots of sexual activity.

4. Sex is simply a form of recreation—nothing more.

Tell It Like It Is

It's our job as parents to counter the current culture. Though frank talk about the sexual messages of media is embarrassing for our sons and for us, we have no choice but to discuss such topics. Boys won't learn morality and what God's Word says about purity by osmosis. They have to be told that the messages they get from the media are not correct. They need to hear about respectful treatment of women, about the dangers of pornography, about filling their minds with the good and with turning away from the evil.

Awesome Alternatives

Got a music lover in your house? Good news! No matter what kind of tunes he craves, there's a Christian band out there who is producing it, selling it, and giving live concerts to promote it.

Say he's a reader. Faith-boosting magazines full of great graphics and hip articles are being published with him in mind. Youth-oriented paperbacks with Christian themes provide great alternatives to less desirable reading material.

If it's video he enjoys...more and more Christian producers are making films wholesome enough to gain your approval, yet packed with enough action, humor, and drama to keep him entertained. Mainstream movies rated G are among the highest box office money-makers. Take advantage of such films. See them in theatres. Buy them on video or DVD to watch at home.

It's not enough for us to simply steer our boys away from inappropriate music, magazines, and TV. Doing so creates a vacuum—one that *will* be filled by something. Theirs is a media-driven culture, and they need high-quality, well-produced material—stuff that is as current and high quality as anything that the world has to offer.

Visit Christian bookstores. Do an on-line search. Talk to Christian leaders who work with teens. Find out from them their best sources of Christian media geared specifically toward youth. It's out there. Lots of it. We are blessed that there are believing artists producing wonderful products, providing us and our sons with valuable, viable alternatives. With just a bit of nudging in the right direction, we can steer our boys away from influences that will hurt and destroy, toward those that will fill their minds and hearts with messages that strengthen, encourage, and uplift.

> *Finally, brothers, whatever is true,*
> *whatever is noble,*
> *whatever is right,*
> *whatever is pure,*
> *whatever is lovely,*
> *whatever is admirable—*
> *if anything is excellent or praiseworthy—*
> *think about such things.*
>
> —PHILIPPIANS 4:8

Great Reviews

1. When a popular Christian band gives a concert in your area, load up your son and three of his friends. Ticket prices are generally reasonable. Many concerts are free. While there, purchase one of the band's T-shirts and a CD for a later surprise gift.

2. Notice your son's reaction to television commercials. When you observe his eyes riveted to the screen during the underwear ads, it's time to have a talk about the false messages that media gives.

3. Talk about ways that Internet sites try to trick kids into giving out personal information. Many on-line contests promise great prizes—for a price. Stress that even when the site appears to be a reliable one, he should not divulge identifying facts about himself. When you come upon a site that tempts you to give out information, show it to him. Explain why you are passing on the opportunity.

11

Time to Sweat

"What's Russell going to be when he gets out of college?" asked Allie, my 12-going-on-13-year-old niece. Allie, her cousin Hannah, who's nine, and I were perched on the high railing of the back deck at Hannah's lakeside house, chatting it up and swinging our feet. It was Christmas day, and the three of us had slipped outside to pass that excruciatingly slow hour between the leisurely eating of Christmas dinner and the frenetic opening of presents.

"He's going to be a teacher. And a coach," I answered.

"Like Uncle Randy?" asked Hannah.

"Yep. Just like Uncle Randy. What do you girls want to be when you grow up?" I asked.

Allie adjusted her cute wire-framed glasses. "A pediatrician."

"Wow, Allie. Really? That's great. You'll be a good pediatrician. Do you like science?"

"Yes. Science is one of my best subjects."

"What about you, Hannah—what do you want to be when you grow up?" I asked.

"I want to work at Sonic."

"Oh?" I struggled not to smile. Allie did too. Sonic is a popular drive-in, fast-food chain in our region. There's a Sonic location in almost every Texas town.

"Uh-huh." Hannah's quick response indicated that she'd given this question lots of thought. I could guess why. An after-school detour to Sonic for soft drinks or ice cream was a special treat that she and her mom enjoyed almost every afternoon. "But I don't want to be the cook and I don't want to be the condiment girl—you know the person who brings you extra napkins and catsup and salt and stuff."

"No. Of course not," Allie and I nodded our understanding. We wouldn't want to be condiment girls either.

"I'm going to be the person who brings people their food and their drinks," said Hannah. I saw a dreamy, faraway look in her eye. "And when my mommy comes to the Sonic and orders her Diet Cherry Coke, I'll be the one who brings it to her. She'll be so surprised to see me!"

Ever since he was old enough to tag along behind his dad to the high school gym for team practices, Russell has known he wanted to be a coach, but somehow, between now and the year she starts college, I expect that Hannah may branch off from her desire to be a carhop at Sonic. Then again, you never know. The girls who work at Sonic do, after all, get to wear roller skates, and precious Hannah... well, she just *loves* to skate!

Just like Dad

Last week, taking a stroll through a quiet neighborhood, I spotted a sight that made me smile. In the front yard of a pretty house were two young men. One of them looked to be around 30 years old. The other appeared to be about four. They were working—hard. Back and forth, back and forth, across the expanse of green grass the two of them trudged. The man was in front, pushing a lawn mower. The little boy, presumably his son, matched him step for step, but stayed several yards behind. He was pushing a lawn mower too—an orange and yellow plastic model, the kind they sell in the toy department at Kmart. The posture of the two guys was identical: arms outstretched, elbows slightly bent, heads down. However, their facial expressions were not the same. Dad's face was blank. I imagine he was eager to get this job done so he could go inside and watch the ball game on TV and enjoy a glass of iced tea.

Not so his little boy. He was pink-cheeked and sweating, but the grin on his face stretched from ear to ear. After all, he was working. Helping his dad. What could be more fun than that?

Allergic to Work

Think such enthusiasm for helping Dad will still be there when that young boy hits adolescence? Don't count on it! Little guys like nothing better than to be given a job, any job—folding wash cloths or picking up sticks will do— but most adolescents are more wary of the working end of a shovel than they are of a snake. They'd rather do almost *anything* than work and can be ingenious in their attempts to get out of it.

Staring up at a cloudless blue sky, an adolescent boy might think, *If I wait long enough—say three or four hours— maybe it'll rain, and I won't be able to paint the fence.*

When confronted by an unhappy mom pointing to a sink full of dishes sitting in cold soapy water, he might think, *Whaddaya mean, I was supposed to rinse, dry, and put away the dishes? That's not what you said. You told me to wash 'em. That's what I did. How was I supposed to know you wanted me to do something else?*

But I did feed the dog. Nobody said anything about water. No matter that the poor pet's tongue is parched and dry.

If these boys displayed the same degree of creativity in other areas of their lives that they do in their attempts to avoid doing chores, there's no telling what they could accomplish in their spare time!

If you are a goal-directed, hard-working, responsible parent, this type of behavior gets *way* under your skin. It drives you nuts to see your son dragging his feet and stalling when it's time to do simple chores. It's difficult not to overreact. Yet does adolescent laziness mean these boys are going to be bums when they grow up? Are they destined to live on welfare? Will they end up standing in soup kitchen lines?

Not likely. The avoidance of work by boys this age is normal and predictable. A lack of initiative and drive is a nearly universal adolescent trait. These qualities are not usually predictors of adult attitudes and behaviors.

Sure, some lazy boys grow up to be men with poor work habits. And yes, parents should begin teaching their boys how to work. Absolutely. But parents should also remember that for almost every boy, this is a developmental stage. And like other stages, it is one that he will pass through.

Walking Willie

When Russell was 11 years old, our family pet was a scruffy little dog named Willie. In an attempt to teach Russell responsibility, Randy and I decided to assign him the chore of feeding, watering, and walking Willie. It would be good for Russell to have a simple job, one that needed to be done every day. Since it would not take more than 15 to 20 minutes of his time, this task seemed tailor-made for an adolescent boy.

At first Russell did his job with little prompting. He liked the fact that Willie depended on him for his breakfast and his dinner. He enjoyed taking Willie for a walk around the block of our quiet neighborhood. No problem. This was a breeze.

But Russell's enthusiasm didn't last long. Within a couple of weeks Randy and I had taken to nagging him daily about taking care of the dog.

"Did you feed Willie yet?"

"No. I will in a minute."

"Russell, Willie doesn't have any water. I thought you gave him some."

"I guess I forgot."

"Russell, haven't you taken Willie for his walk? It's almost dark outside."

"I meant to."

As weeks went by, Randy and I grew more and more irritated with Russell for not taking proper care of the dog. Our plan to teach him more responsibility wasn't working. So we decided to take a different approach.

"Russell, from now on we are not going to remind you to take care of Willie. You are on your own. It will be up to you to remember to give him food and water and to take him on his walk. No more reminders. Understand?"

Sure Russell understood. That sounded like a great plan. What was all the fuss about anyway? He didn't need to be reminded. Really. He didn't.

There was just one catch, we warned. Willie had to be taken care of every single day.

No problem, Russell assured us.

The next day, Russell came home from school, watched some TV, went to soccer practice, ate dinner, did some homework, took his bath, and went to bed. No food for Willie. No water and no walk.

Randy and I, watching the late show, waited until he had been asleep for an hour. We went to his room. "Russell," Randy called his name. "Hop up. You've got to go take care of Willie."

I pulled back the covers.

Russell rubbed his eyes, sat up in bed, and looked at us like we were nuts. "What time is it?"

"Eleven-thirty."

"And I gotta take Willie for a walk *now?*"

"Did you do it earlier?"

"I guess I forgot."

"Then yep. He needs his walk. Hop up and get your clothes on."

It's *dark* at eleven-thirty at night. Dark and a little bit scary. Stumbling along behind your dog when everyone else on the street is asleep is not fun. (Russell never knew it, but to ensure his safety, Randy followed a ways behind, staying out of sight.)

When Russell got home, he poured Willie some food and headed back to bed.

Soon as he was snuggled in, I went to his room and turned on the light. "Did you give him water?"

He groaned.

You would think that a single nocturnal trip around the block would motivate a kid to do his job in a timely manner. Not so our bright boy. It took getting awakened five nights out of the next seven for Russell to finally get the idea. But once he did, we never had to remind him to take care of Willie again.

As for Willie? He was sure glad when Russell finally got the idea. It was no fun for him to have to wake up and trek around the block in the middle of the night either. Supper or no supper, he too would have rather stayed in bed!

Chore Time

Despite boys' natural tendencies to loaf, when they are assigned regular chores, the entire family benefits. Being required to perform a routine job teaches boys responsibility. They learn that work is an important and necessary part of life.

Kids who grow up in rural settings (like my brothers and I did) routinely help out by caring for livestock and by planting, tending, and harvesting crops. Their help is truly needed and appreciated. Work for them is a natural and vital extension of family life. Boys whose families own their own businesses are in the same situation. The help of each family member is both expected and required. During busy times, everyone is expected to pitch in.

However, most sons, like Russell, don't grow up on farms or ranches. Family-owned businesses are not the norm. In the majority of homes, Mom and Dad go somewhere else to work. The family homestead is a suburban house on a half- to quarter-acre lot. It's not uncommon for busy professional families to employ someone to help with both the housework and the yard work. With all of this outside help, how much work is left for a boy to do?

Honestly, not a lot. Yet, for their good, we need to assign them jobs. Most of the time it would be infinitely easier to take care of things ourselves or hire work out. Yet time spent assigning chores and seeing that they get done is valuable to the development of our boys. Here are a few of the chores that we assigned Russell to do at various times (in addition to taking care of the dog).

1. Take out the garbage

2. Mow the yard

3. Rake and bag leaves

4. Do his own laundry

5. Clean up the kitchen after making himself a snack

6. Wash the cars and clean out the inside

7. Baby-sit his sister while we went out

Every Fall They Fall

Of all the jobs assigned to him when he was living at home, Russell disliked raking and bagging the leaves the most (so did we). At the time, we lived in a country house situated on a huge lot that was graced with more than three dozen leaf-dropping trees. Every fall, it was an unpleasant ordeal to get Russell to rake and bag those leaves. After shooing him out the door, I'd stand at the window and watch. He would rake a bit, stop, stand, and look up at the sky (praying for rain, I guessed). Then he'd rake a bit more, stop, scratch, check his fingernails, rake a bit more, then come in for a drink. This would go on for hours...for days. A job that should have filled every afternoon for a week always stretched into a torturous month-long ordeal because of Russell's procrastination.

Randy and I had to stay on him every day to get the job done and to do it right. Because he didn't fill the leaf bags full, stubbornly insisting that they were as full as he could get them, he required three times as many bags as were really necessary to get the job done. Often, rather than bagging as he went, Russell would rake up ten or so tall piles of leaves, explaining that first he would rake, then he would bag. Of course, when a big wind came up, his piles scattered and he had to rake again. Sometimes, when he had gotten around to the bagging, he wouldn't get the tops closed securely enough. The bags would pop open, scattering leaves, and he'd have to rake and bag them again.

Seeing to it that Russell got the task done, and listening to him complain, stall, and make excuses, was *no fun*. In that little rural community, we could have easily hired someone to come rake and bag the leaves for about $30. Honestly, avoiding the yearly ordeal of hassling Russell to get the job done would have been worth $100 at least! Yet being required to accomplish a long, tedious, and lonely task was good for Russell. It taught him that the only way to finish a task is to stick with it. He learned that doing a job correctly on the first attempt saves time.

There was also an added benefit to our requirement that Russell accomplish this annual task—one that neither Randy nor I expected. Having to rake those leaves all those years inspired Russell to do well in school. No way did he want to grow up and tend yards for a living! There's another thing too: Russell says that when he's grown and has a home of his own, his yard will be full of sunshine, for he plans to have no trees!

Work's Not Punishment

At the time that Russell was required rake all of those leaves, it probably felt to him like the worst form of punishment. After all, if you don't want to do it, and you have to do it anyway, it must be punishment. Right?

Wrong. Randy and I assigned Russell the task for two reasons. First, the leaves needed to be raked. Second, Russell needed to learn how to work. We did not give him the job because he had done something wrong. In our home we don't give jobs in response to misbehavior. There are more effective and more appropriate ways to discipline, such as grounding or imposing restrictions on the use of TV, music, or the computer.

When parents assign chores or jobs as a means of punishment, it gives sons the unintentional message that work is unpleasant and something to be avoided. Is that the way we want our boys to look at work? As something to be avoided, something to be dreaded, and something to try to behave your way out of?

Of course not. Though many of us have days when we dread going to our jobs, we know that work is not a punitive action imposed upon our lives. Neither should we, by our actions, impose such a belief on our boys.

Lessons in Work

Our goal as parents is to see our boys mature into productive adults—men who view work as a necessary and enjoyable part of their lives. Our hope for them is that when they grow up and choose their vocations, they will find something to do that is challenging and fulfilling— jobs they can take pride in doing well.

Our work may be white-, blue-, or pink-collar; we may do it away from the home or at home. If we view it as a blessing for which we are thankful, our sons will view work as something positive. They will take their cues from us. Randy's prayers before family meals often include thanks for the means that he and I have to provide for the material needs of our family. This lets our children know that we view our jobs as something for which to be thankful.

Do we give our kids the impression that we love everything about our jobs every single day? No way. Both Russell and his sister, Rachel, are aware that sometimes there are problems and some days their mom and dad would much rather play than work. We have both held jobs that were difficult and unpleasant. Our children have heard us complain! But they've also seen us go to work anyway. Our hope is to show them that even when they are required to do a job that they don't enjoy (such as raking leaves!) it's possible to do it with a good attitude.

Teaching these boys of ours to have good work ethics is important for them and for us. After all, our hope is that they will have good jobs and be able to support us in style when, years from now, we, their beloved parents, are old, decrepit, and gray!

Time to punch that clock!

Moreover, when God gives any man wealth and possessions, and enables him to enjoy them, to accept his lot and be happy in his work—this is a gift of God.

—ECCLESIASTES 5:19

Work and Play

1. There's an official Take Your Daughter to Work Day, yet no similar special day is set aside for sons. That's too bad. Boys benefit from spending time with their parents at work too. Plan a special day to take your son with you. He'll enjoy seeing what you do at your job.

2. Some chores are meant to be shared. Boys who hate to toil alone enjoy spending time working with their parents. Painting and cleaning out rain gutters are two jobs that are best done in tandem.

3. If your son shows particular interest in a career different from your own, such as firefighting, engineering, or even serving as a chef in a fancy restaurant, arrange for him to spend time with a man who does that job. Even a couple of hours spent at a specific job site can give him a greater understanding of a profession—especially if it's one that you know little about.

12
Making the Team

When Russell was four years old, his dad and I signed him up for community league soccer. We'd never played soccer, never even *watched* soccer, so neither Randy nor I knew much about the game.

The first thing we learned that season was that early spring soccer was a *cold* sport! After Russell's first game, we decided that the treeless soccer field complex in our town had to be among the chilliest places on earth. Still, being devoted fans and proud parents, every Saturday morning we'd bundle up and arrive at the soccer field with our folding lawn chairs, blankets, and thermos bottles of hot chocolate.

It's funny—the icy winds never seemed to bother the little guys on the teams. They spurned their mothers' attempts to wrap them up in blankets between quarters. A few of them would give in and wear thermal underwear beneath their uniforms, but no way was any one of them willing to put sweat pants on over his shorts.

They insisted they weren't even cold.

It didn't take Randy and me long to figure out that, at this age, there weren't too many strategies involved in winning a game. The teams played quarters with short breaks in between. We loved to eavesdrop on the coach's between-quarters instructions. They generally went something like this.

Coach: "Okay boys, which way are we going to kick the ball *this* time?"

Team: "That way!" (Half the boys would be pointing to the right, half to the left. At least one would be picking his nose.)

Coach: "Come on fellas. Listen up. We're gonna run *this* way. Got it? *This* way. Okay? Everybody ready to win?"

Team: "Yeah!"

Coach: "Okay then. All set? Let's go play!"

Team: "Wait! Coach! Wait! When do we get our juice boxes?"

Randy and I had lots of fun watching and learning that season. Some of what we saw was a hoot. One of Russell's best friends got to be the goalie that year. He did pretty well except for the one time when, bored, he passed the time weaving his hands and arms in and out of the net. When the ball came toward him, he was so tangled up that he couldn't free himself and the other team scored a goal.

Many Saturdays, we watched as several of the boys, Russell included, forgot about the game, opting instead to sit down and dig in the dirt. Others chased butterflies and bugs.

Unfortunately—for the coaches anyway—the community soccer fields were located right next to a railroad track. If you've got a son, you probably remember that there is not much that fascinates a little boy more than a train. These junior athletes were no exception. Every time the train went by, blowing its whistle and clanging its bell, parents, coaches, and referees knew to expect all action on the field to screech to a stop. The boys would freeze wherever they were on the field and stand transfixed and slack jawed until the last car of the train had passed. Only then would the game resume.

Competition's Where It's At

I admit I don't miss those frigid Saturday mornings spent at the soccer fields. I enjoy sleeping in, munching on a leisurely breakfast, and reading the newspaper in the warmth of my home. However, I do miss the long-gone attitude of nonchalance with which those cute little tykes played.

The mind-set of being more concerned with butterflies and juice boxes than with scoring the winning goal doesn't last long. At four years old, Russell's friends on that long-ago team were enjoying some of the last days of such play. Quickly, so quickly, a peculiarly masculine drive to win kicks in.

Masculine? Yes. Some girls like to compete, and yes, *some* like to compete *a lot,* but it's not the same. Randy has made a career of coaching girls. In *most* cases, he says, girls don't have the same drive to win that boys do. Randy's observed that on a long bus trip home after losing a big game, within minutes of boarding, a team of girls will be chatting, singing, and acting silly with each other. A losing boy's team, on the other hand, will quietly sulk and stay mad at themselves and each other the entire trip home. Winning or losing is just not as big a deal to most girls as it is to most boys. Many girls, even athletic, ball-playing girls, do not have extremely competitive natures.

Rarely is that true of a boy. Competition is a fact of life for most males. Even if he's a lazy, laid-back, easy-going kid, he still loves to compete—perhaps not in athletics, but when it comes to band, academics, or the cool way that he dresses, watch out! He will believe that *he is the man.* If he's a quiet boy, it may be easy to miss, but watch and listen—you'll see that the need to win or one-up those around him permeates almost everything he does.

This competitive nature is present all through a male's life, but the desire to compete is especially fierce in adolescent boys. From who gets to sit where in the family van to who can eat the most pancakes and whose breath stinks the worst, a boy will find some way to turn most any of life's little details into some kind of contest.

I'm no anthropologist and no expert on human behavior. However, there are lots of folks who seek to explain this inborn, cross-cultural, manly drive to win. Perhaps, like many of them say, it's part of God's plan. Competitive, driven men may be more willing and able to protect and defend their families.

To me, that sounds like as reasonable an explanation as any.

One thing's for sure. Any parent who tries to teach, train, or discipline away a son's drive to compete is going to get discouraged quickly. For an adolescent boy, it's all about winning. He wants to prove he's the biggest, best, strongest, smartest, and most powerful.

King of the mountain? That's who our sons long to be. Sports provide many boys with opportunities to at least try to be king.

Good for the Mind and the Body

Athletic participation provides active, energetic boys with acceptable ways to utilize their natural, healthy tendencies toward aggression, adventure, and risk taking. They learn discipline, concentration, and, in team sports, cooperation and concern for others.

Obesity is epidemic in America today. It's a growing problem for adults and adolescents. Becoming physically fit through participation in a sport sets a boy on a lifelong path toward healthier living.

Exercise relieves stress. When much of his life feels unpredictable and out of control, lacing up a pair of sneakers and hitting the pavement is a great way to let off steam. Boys concerned with staying active and fit may be less likely to smoke, drink alcohol, or use drugs. Boys who are shy and don't make friends easily find camaraderie and friendship on an athletic team. When I asked former student athlete, Jamie, now a college freshman, what it was he missed most about high school, he quickly told me it was the experience of being on an athletic team. He missed being a part of a group of guys whose goal was focused on winning the next game.

Team Sports

Many little boys dream about the day when they will be old enough to play on a team. They can't wait to claim a uniform and a coach. They believe that practices and games will be the most fun thing they have ever done.

For almost every sport, there's a team to join. Baseball, soccer, and football are common. Some towns have swim teams, youth tennis leagues, even hockey for kids. To locate a team in a sport that interests your son, ask around. Question parents who have older boys, watch the newspaper, call your town's parks and recreation department or the local YMCA. Most youth sports programs are well managed, but before signing him up, there are a few things a parent should check out.

What to Look for in a Youth Sports Organization

1. Organization. Look for a knowledgeable, in-charge person (even if that person is a volunteer) to be available to answer your questions. Ask for rules and guidelines in writing. Are game days and practice

schedules set in advance? When are those schedules available to parents? Are parents welcome to attend practices?

2. Safety. Teams should be divided according to age or size. Look to see if well-maintained safety equipment is being used consistently. Players should be taught to use all equipment safely. No horseplay should be allowed.

3. Good coaches. They should be screened and knowledgeable about their sport. They need to have the ability to keep their teams disciplined and under control. Most important of all, coaches should love kids more than they love the game.

4. Sportsmanship. Bad manners and poor sportsmanship should not be tolerated. Coaches should both model good sportsmanship and demand it from their players.

5. Fun. Kids who play ought to be having a great time. Even if your son isn't a starter for the team, at this age he should get to play at least a part of every game.

Should You Bail?

The majority of adults who coach youth sports do so because they love to hang out with kids and they love the sport. Most are kind, responsible, levelheaded people. They spend long hours teaching kids how to play and have fun for no pay and little recognition. Sadly, it is the rare coach who behaves inappropriately who gets the press.

Chances are, your son will have a great experience playing youth sports. He'll most likely be coached by someone he will like and respect. However, if his coach repeatedly affects him in a negative way by cursing, belittling players, or failing to insist on safe play, schedule a time to talk with the coach. If he or she is not receptive to your concerns, take the problem up with the head of the organization. Ask that your son be placed on a different team. If all else fails, remove him from the team. No, we don't want our sons to be quitters, yet they are still *children* who are worthy of our parental interventions on their behalf.

A Team of One

Even boys who have no desire to play team sports can enjoy the benefits of athletic activities. Your son may not like football or baseball. He may love roller blading, mountain bike riding, golf, or skateboarding. Great! Encourage him. Learn about his chosen sport. Make sure he keeps his gear well maintained and that he uses proper safety equipment at all times. Participation in most individual sports will almost guarantee that he will meet guys who share his interests.

One of the biggest benefits of individual sport participation is that a boy who's late to grow tall and strong or one who loves athletics but lacks the natural talent needed to make the school team has a chance to compete—against himself. Trying to outdo his personal best ensures success and increased discipline and self-esteem.

Winning's Fun

What a great feeling it is to be the winner! Fans cheer, the coach smiles, and somebody's dad treats everyone to ice cream. Sometimes there's a trophy or a ribbon to display at home. When your son wins an athletic competition, celebrate with him. Compliment him on his play.

Point out specifically what he did well. This is his time to shine.

Talk to your son about how to be a good winner. Hopefully coaches will insist that the teams shake hands. Losers should congratulate winners, but winners need to be taught to tell the losing team that they played a good game. Make sure he understands that while celebrating his own win is great, he should never ever make fun of opposing players.

Losing Stinks

Often, it's the luck of the draw. Even though league organizers *thought* they had the talent evenly divided, your son's team ended up with no boys who can hit while the other teams are stacked with half a dozen guys who are big for their ages, are shadow-lipped, and who can hit the ball over the fence half the time.

Sooner or later, if he plays long enough, every boy is going to end up on a losing team. And even if it's not a season when his team keeps getting beat, every boy, even an extremely athletic one, is going to mess up eventually. He may even be the last-second cause of his team losing.

Getting whipped every week isn't fun. Messing up is embarrassing. Even if the team is doing okay, it's hard to keep your chin up if you're the goalie who gets scored on every time the coach gets brave and puts you in. The older a boy gets, the more losing bothers him. Yet losing teaches valuable lessons. Boys learn about not giving up when the going gets tough, about doing their best even when your best is lousy, and about the importance of team unity.

If he's having an off year, either personally or as a team, encourage him. Point out ways he and his team are improving, even if they aren't winning. Insist he stick it out. When he blames the officials or other members of his team for losses—and he will—listen while he blows off steam. When he's calmed down, explain why such talk is inappropriate. Point out that everyone is doing their best. It's never okay to argue with or blame officials for a loss.

Without a doubt, those losing seasons are long ones. No one likes them. Yet being on a losing team provides great opportunities for adolescent character building. Besides, there's always next year!

Just for Fun

Some of the best times kids can have are during simple neighborhood games. During his middle school years, Russell, being one of the oldest kids on the block, was the ringleader of a summertime crew of neighborhood boys. The group of nine guys ranged in age from 8 to 13. Our quiet, safe neighborhood provided a place for the boys to roam, romp, and play. Though mothers up and down the block remained unseen, their eagle eyes kept tabs on their sons' actions, and those boys enjoyed hours of freedom, uninterrupted by adults.

The crew of boys held races and contests to see who could launch their bikes the farthest off of flimsy ramps they built by propping up pieces of scavenged scrap plywood on bricks pilfered from their garages. They constructed a vacant lot clubhouse and sneaked snacks for each other from mothers known to keep well-stocked pantries.

One summer they made their own baseball field. Every afternoon for a week the boys worked on clearing the weedy, rocky, overgrown field behind our house. They mowed. They raked. They picked up sticks. And when they were done, did they ever have fun! More fun, I'd venture to guess, than any of them ever had playing on any organized team. No uniforms, no umpires, no fans. Just a bunch of sweaty boys having a great time.

Unorganized play, whether it be sandlot baseball, hoops shot in the driveway, or touch (yeah right!) football in someone's backyard, is an activity every boy should have the opportunity to enjoy. Mixing it up with guys of different ages and abilities takes away lots of the pressure present in league sports. Encourage such homegrown play. Keep basic equipment available, including aired-up balls so that your son and his friends can play on a moment's notice. Kids who have no hopes or desires to play on an organized team can enjoy friendly street games. If there's room, put a basketball hoop in your driveway and invite the neighborhood kids to use it any time they want. Who knows—maybe they'll even invite you, Mom and Dad, to play too!

Do you not know that in a race all the runners run,
but only one gets the prize?
Run in such a way as to get the prize.
Everyone who competes in the games goes into strict training.
They do it to get a crown that will not last;
but we do it to get a crown that will last forever.

—1 CORINTHIANS 9:24-25

Let the Games Begin

1. Encourage your son to try a new sport. If he's always played on a team, he might enjoy trying an individual athletic endeavor like karate or skiing.

2. Watch pro games together. Point out players whose sideline or end zone behaviors are inappropriate. Discuss the consequences of arguing with an official. Talk about appropriate ways to celebrate good plays.

3. Attend local sporting events as a family. High school games are inexpensive and lots of fun.

4. Encourage your son to play sports he can enjoy for a lifetime such as golf, tennis, or running. This sets the course for future fitness.

13

But I'm Broke!

Video game rentals.

Convenience store snacks on the walk home from school.

High-priced, over-budget—*way over-budget*—athletic shoes.

Music CDs.

Concert T-shirts.

Computer games.

Professional sports team caps.

The tally of material goodies that adolescent boys crave goes on and on. Thanks to advertisements aimed especially at them, their list of wants and perceived needs is a long one. And the price tags attached to these goods?

Cha-ching. Cha-ching.

Nothing's cheap.

We adults like stuff, but our boys need no help from us when it comes to developing a desire for material things. Like hungry birds in a nest, they call out for more and more. Sure, it's our jobs to provide for our sons, but what our boys *really* need from us are healthy attitudes toward material possessions. They also need us to teach them how to both make their money and manage it.

In Favor of an Allowance

I agree with the experts who advocate the giving of an allowance—cash given for the sole purpose of teaching kids to budget and manage their funds. When Russell was in elementary school, his dad and I began doling out a preset amount of cash at the beginning of each week. Russell's allowance consisted of the money that we would normally give him on a daily or weekly basis for things like school lunches and supplies, club activities and dues, and ball game concessions. To that amount we added a couple of extra dollars. By receiving money regularly and before he needed it, Russell learned how to make money last—most of the time! I suspect he suffered through a few hungry middle school lunches after splurging on too many after-school snacks early in the week.

When Russell got into high school, his needs increased, so the amount we gave him increased too. We also began giving him his allowance every two weeks instead of every one so that he could learn even better how to manage his available funds

Russell's allowance was not tied to his behavior or to chores. If he got himself into trouble, his allowance did not get cut. If he did something extra nice, he didn't get a bonus. When he wanted money for something his allowance did not cover, he worked, either for us, doing jobs we would have paid someone else to do, or at a job in the community.

The system worked well for us. It simplified Randy's life and mine because we no longer found ourselves hunting and scrounging for needed cash on a daily basis. Russell liked not having to ask for lunch money every day. Most of the time he handled his spending in a mature way. When he didn't do so well, he suffered the consequences, though occasionally, because he was still learning, we bailed him out of financial jams.

Secret Stash

My neighbor Kelly believes in teaching her kids to do their own laundry. She's got three boys, all of them in their teens. Over the years, Kelly's made it a ritual of sorts. Shortly after each boy's twelfth birthday, she presents him with his own laundry basket and a detailed lesson on how to properly wash clothes. In case a boy forgets, she's posted typed instructions on how to sort clothes, the correct amount of soap to use, and what temperature of water to select depending on whether the load is of whites or of colors. Her boys, after age 12, are responsible for the washing, drying, folding, and putting away of their clothes, sheets, and towels. For the task of taking care of their clothes, she pays them eight dollars a week.

Kelly's proud of herself. She believes she's getting a great deal. She's a busy, working mom, so it's worth it to her to pay her boys for helping with a chore that she would normally do herself. Besides, by teaching her sons to do laundry, Kelly figures she's racking up points with her future daughters-in-law.

I have to grin when I remember how all has not always gone according to Kelly's efficient plan. Last year when she and her family moved into a new home, Kelly replaced her thin, ragged bath towels with some spanking new, oversized fluffy ones—a whopping dozen color-coordinated sets for each of her home's three bathrooms. An abundant, luxurious stash of towels was something Kelly had wanted for a long time. Never again did she plan on running out of towels or being embarrassed when hosting overnight guests.

Strange thing was, only two months after their move, Kelly began noticing a chronic shortage of the navy and cream towels that her son Tommy used in his bathroom. "What do you mean, you don't know where they are?" she asked him. "Didn't you do laundry yesterday? How come there are only three towels in the cabinet?"

Tommy had no idea.

None?

At least none that he cared to share.

Seems the location of the missing towels was quite a puzzle. No one had taken towels to Boy Scout camp. No one had borrowed towels for a fund-raising car wash. No one had taken them outside to use to wash the dog. Where else could they be?

Several weeks into the mystery of the missing towels, as Kelly was digging in Tommy's closet for a sleeping bag, she figured out exactly where they could be. She was furious when she discovered, rather *uncovered,* a stinky stash of damp mildewed towels hidden in the back corner of the closet.

Tommy had no good explanation for why the towels were there save that he had been too tired to do all that washing. In his mind, throwing them in the back of his closet had been easier than simply tossing them in the washing machine. He had intended to do them. Really he had.

When?

Why, later, of course.

The funny thing was, Tommy hadn't been too tired to spend the eight dollars a week he had been getting paid to do a job he hadn't done. Not too tired at all! However, by the time he finished all of the work his angry mom lined up for him to do to pay her back, the boy had a much better idea of what *tired* felt like.

Motivated to Work

Adolescents can be full of energy and eager to please. They can also be among the laziest creatures God put on this earth! We want our boys to grow up to be energetic, productive workers. We expect them to some day obtain good jobs and work hard to support themselves and their families. Reconciling those desires with the reality of a boy who will sleep until noon if we let him, who will slide dirty dishes under his bed to keep from having to make a trip to the kitchen, and who would rather use his foot to smash down the trash in the can than take it out makes us nuts.

So what's the best thing we can use to motivate our sons to work—to do chores beyond those normally expected of contributing members of a household?

No surprise—it's the same thing that motivates us adults to get up, get dressed, and head out the door most Monday mornings. Money! When prompted by the desire to make money, lazy boys have been known to get up off the couch and to occasionally even break a sweat. But there's a key to lighting this fire beneath their slow-moving behinds. The desire to make money will motivate only if a boy wants something he cannot obtain without a stash of cash of his own. After all, if he has everything he wants, why should he work?

To Give or Hold Back

Ours is an affluent society. Even those boys growing up in homes where money is tight rarely *need* anything they don't have. We parents love to please our kids. There is nothing that gives us more joy than seeing their faces light up when we give them something they truly want. When parents have the financial ability to give their boys not only what they need, but also most all of what they want, it can feel heartless, unreasonable, and even *unnatural* to with-hold some of the extra goodies that they desire. Yet is it?

Let's take a look.

When a boy is given everything he longs for without working for it, he learns little about the value of money. However, if he works four hours on a Saturday morning, then spends his entire morning's earnings that afternoon on a movie and snacks, he learns a valuable lesson. Goods and services are not free. Money represents time expended.

If he works to earn some of his own spending money, he will appreciate those things that he buys more than if they were given to him. More than one parent, upon suggesting to a son that he purchase a particular requested item with his own money, has been amused to hear that son say, "Never mind. I don't want it that bad." It's funny how these boys of ours want things really badly if we are paying for them, yet their desire for those same items wanes when they contemplate spending their own hard-earned cash!

There is worth and lasting value to be found in the process of waiting for something, pride to be gained by a son who earns something he wants without help from his parents. Unwittingly, we can deprive our son of lessons more important and lasting than the latest garment, gadget, or piece of gear he craves. To long for something, to plan and save for it, and to finally accomplish the goal of getting that item is a delicious experience for adults and kids alike. Often, it is in the waiting and anticipating that the most joy is found.

What do you give and what do you make him earn on his own? Those are choices for individual families to make. What in our family are considered extras—items that a child should earn if he wants—would be considered necessities in other families, goods that should absolutely be provided by parents. There's no rule. Parents should practice what feels right for them and their sons—as long as there is *something* left for a boy to obtain on his own.

A concept that has worked extremely well for our family is what we call the choice of an upgrade. Say a son needs new jeans and wants a particularly expensive brand. His parents don't care to spend that much on jeans, so they agree to provide the funds for a basic, less costly pair. The difference in the price of the two jeans is what the son would be expected to pitch in.

How badly does he want the more pricey pair?

Badly enough to use his own earnings?

Sometimes. But many times not.

Entertainment is one of those extras that sons can contribute some of their own money to. Obviously, if the whole family is going to an amusement park or a movie, we aren't going to leave him at home if he's broke. It's right that parents pay for such treats. However, if he wants to attend an expensive concert or ball game with friends, it might be a good idea to have him earn or save the money for his ticket and food.

Me—Work?

In order for a boy to *have* money, he's got to find ways to *earn* money. And who better to be his first boss than his mom and his dad? I see nothing wrong with paying a son to do things that we would pay someone else to do for us. If Mom has a housekeeper who comes in once a week and a son wants the job, why not give him a chance? The same goes for hiring him to help with painting or window washing. As long as we treat the arrangement as a business deal and hold him to the same high standard that we would someone else, a homegrown arrangement can benefit both him and us.

Still needing funds? Lots of opportunities are available for even preteen boys to earn money. If he's a hard worker, or at least a worker who tries hard, and if he has a touch of creativity and imagination, your son can find work right in your neighborhood.

Jobs for Boys

1.　Mowing lawns—an oldie but still a goodie. The demand for dependable boys to mow, rake, edge, and weed yards has never been higher. Busy families are eager to hire boys to take care of their yards on a regular or occasional basis.

2.　Garage and storeroom cleanup. People need help with once-a-year jobs. A boy will get the best response if he offers this service in the spring when folks are in the mood to get rid of excess stuff.

3.　Pet care. Boarding a pet while on vacation is expensive. Many pet owners will gladly pay someone to feed, water, and walk their pet while they are gone for a few days.

4.　Computer lessons. Many boys are adept at working with computers. If he knows what he's doing, he can make money by offering, for an hourly fee, to help new computer owners set up their machines and learn basic tasks like e-mail and word processing.

5.　Produce a neighborhood newsletter. Using a personal computer, an imaginative kid can produce a weekly newsletter that families in his neighborhood will enjoy reading. He can include neighborhood news, birthdays and anniversaries, a listing of lost and found items, want ads, and even recipes from noted neighborhood cooks. If a young man came to my door selling such a rag, I'd gladly shell out a dollar—and I think most folks would.

The Big Bad "B" Word

Many adults have yet to master the art of budgeting. Perhaps, like me, you weren't taught how to divvy up money so that things come out right at the end of the month. It's true. At our house, we almost always run out of money before we run out of month! Many of us hope that our children will manage money better than we do.

When teaching your son how to budget, a simple envelope system is likely to work best. Prepare three sturdy envelopes. Label one Save, one Church or Charity, and one Spend. Teach your son that every time he receives money other than his allowance, such as his birthday money or cash he makes mowing yards, he is to place 10 percent into savings and to set 10 percent aside for his giving. Once he's done that, the remaining 80 percent is his to spend as he chooses.

Allow your son to spend his 80 percent any way he decides—even if his choice of consumer goods seems foolish and shortsighted. As for the savings, agree ahead of time how often he will be allowed to dip into that envelope. Once every three months is reasonable for a younger boy, once every six months for an older one. Encourage him to think of something special he wants to save toward. Working for a financial goal is great preparation for the saving and spending he'll be doing when he's an adult.

Bottom Line

It's a fact of our modern life. How much money we have, what we do with it, and how we manage it affects every aspect of our lives. Good money management brings with it certain freedoms. Investing the time necessary to teach a boy good management prepares him to manage the funds of his household when he is a man.

There's an added benefit too. If we do our jobs well, who knows? Some day when we're in a pinch, perhaps we'll be able to talk our sons into giving us loans!

Dishonest money dwindles away,
but he who gathers money little by little makes it grow.

—PROVERBS 13:11

Money Matters

1. Take your son with you when you grocery shop. Show him how to read the price per unit label displayed below each product. Compare cereal prices, looking at the kind sold in a bag, the store's brand, and those bearing a national name brand. Ask him to pretend he has ten dollars to spend on cereal. Which product would he buy? Why? How long would it last?

2. Tell your son when you are saving for a particular item. Let him know the ways you are cutting back in order to reach your savings goal.

3. Hold a family garage sale. Ask everyone to help out and see that all family members benefit. Use the proceeds from the garage sale for a weekend trip or outing.

4. As a family, do something extra for a local charity. Collect change in a jar on the counter. Once every three months, donate the amount to a homeless shelter. Skip dinner one night a week. Use the money you would have spent on food to purchase groceries for a community food bank.

14
Like Father, Like Son

My husband, Randy, looks exactly like his mother.

My son, Russell, looks exactly like his dad. They have the same nose, the same mouth, and the same eyes—hazel, long lashes, heavy brows. The two of them look so much alike that except for the proof-positive stretch marks that zigzag across my tummy, no one would guess that I had anything to do with the bringing of my own son into this world.

Not only does Russell look like his dad, their personalities are almost identical too. They both possess calm, easygoing, laid-back temperaments. They both love to sleep late and like nothing better than to spend a lazy Saturday afternoon watching sports on TV. When we go out to eat, both Randy and Russell can be counted on to order chicken-fried steaks and french fries nine times out of ten. Their voices sound so much alike that since Russell turned 14, folks calling our house have been unable to tell if they were speaking to the older or the younger of the two Smith men. Randy and Russell walk like each other. They both squint and shield their eyes with their right arms when they're forced to look into the sun. The two of them even sit and stand alike—usually you'll find them both leaned up against a wall.

When I run into folks who know Russell's in college, often they ask me how he's doing and what he plans to do with his life.

"Russell? Doing fine. Pretty much wants to *be* his dad," I tell them. "He would like to have his dad's life." So far, that's true. Our firstborn is on track to become a teacher and a coach like his dad. He'd like to get married as soon as he gets out of school—just like his dad. Having two kids, a boy then a girl, would suit Russell just fine.

Perfection? Not Hardly!

Is Randy, the man Russell emulates, a perfect man?

A perfect dad?

Far from it. He'd tell you so himself. No dad gets it right all of the time, nor is a son's imitation of his father dependent upon perfection. Whether he's an attentive involved dad, or one who is aloof and out of his son's life for big chunks of time, there is an ingredient in a boy's makeup that causes him to strive to imitate his dad. Most boys desire to be, and *will* grow up to be, much like their fathers in many ways. They'll pick up their fathers' good qualities as well as some of their flaws and imperfections.

My bet is that though your son and his dad may not have a strong physical resemblance or possess similar temperaments like Randy and Russell do, you still see amazing father–son similarities. It's also a good bet that the older your son gets, the more glimpses of his dad you'll see in him.

Dad Is the Man

It starts when our sons are toddlers. Seems that as soon as they're out of their mom's arms, little boys start trying to fill their dad's shoes. Sure, Mother's the one they go to for cuddles and comforts. They'll always love and need her. But being males, they especially relate to and long to be like their dads.

God made boys this way. Imitation is the way all humans learn how to behave. Think about it. Adults in new social situations observe other adults for clues as to how to act and react. Girls watch their mothers. They identify with them. By watching and listening, they learn how to be women. Boys do the same with their dads.

Society would have us believe that dads are not important, that once conception takes place, a man's job is done. Popular media portrays most fathers as being drags on their families. Dad's a joke at best; mean, ignorant, and abusive at worst. Rarely is a dad seen as being a strong, intelligent, and contributing part of his wife and children's lives.

That view is not accurate. Dads are vitally important to their families. Girls need their dads—of course they do. (I devoted an entire chapter in *Help! My Little Girl's Growing Up* to the importance of a dad in a daughter's life.) But it is boys, especially adolescent boys, whose development is most strongly related to their relationships with their dads. Sons look to their dads to see exactly what they are supposed to become.

Apron Strings No More

When a boy nears adolescence, his relationship with his mother changes. He still loves her and needs her, and he should most certainly be required to behave respectfully toward her. Yet no longer does he identify with her in the same way that he did when he was little. Most moms feel their sons pulling away from them during the adolescent years. Those of us who don't know it's coming often get our feelings hurt. What's happening? We fear we're losing our little boys. And in a sense, we are. Yet what we're gaining is a young man. This slight pulling back from Mom is normal and healthy, a sign that he is growing to be the man that God will have him become.

A boy is separating himself not just from his mother but from his identification with all things female. It is now toward his dad and other men that he looks to learn about masculinity and manhood. When he focuses increased attention on his dad, he is seeing what a man is supposed to look like and how a man is expected to act.

Adolescent boys need men in their lives. No matter how good a parent she aims to be, it is impossible for a mom to teach her son how to be a man. Mothers make great moms, but they make terrible men!

Missing in Action

Where does this leave single moms? What about the many families that have two parents living in the same house but a dad who is not engaged in the life of the family? How does a mom handle that difficult situation? What's a mom to do if her husband and her son simply don't click? What does she do if, because of personality conflicts and divergent interests, they can barely tolerate each other?

Simple answer, yet not simple at all: She does the best that she can.

Dads are important. A male influence is vital. That fact can't be denied. Yet many single moms rear terrific sons. Most boys who live in single-parent homes—or even homes where Dad doesn't do his part—turn out just fine.

Whenever possible, smooth the way for your son to have a relationship with his dad—whether or not you all live together in the same house. A boy may want to begin spending more time with his dad than he has in times past. Encourage it. Speak well of his dad to your son and speak well of your son to his dad. If there are misunderstandings between them, be the peacemaker. Try to help them understand each other's views.

Many sons of divorced parents decide they want to go live with their dads about the time they reach adolescence. Each case is unique, but prayerfully taking into account how much a boy this age needs his dad, some families decide a move may be the right thing. Seek wise counsel if you are uneasy or unsure about such a change.

If a son is rejected by his dad, do not resort to putdowns and blame, but let your son know that it is his dad who is making the mistake—a mistake that has nothing to do with him. Make sure that he knows he is valuable and loved. If a son needs counseling, seek it out for him. Look for a Christian professional with experience in the care of adolescents. Feelings of rejection can lead to depression, aggression, and rebellious behavior. Get him whatever help he needs.

Seek out male relationships for your son to enjoy. Boy Scout leaders, church youth group leaders, coaches, teachers, and extended family members can provide great masculine role models. Regular time spent with "the guys" will be something that your son looks forward to; those will be hours that can have a lasting impact on his development into a man.

Just Hangin' Out

It's tough being an attentive dad in these busy times. Many aspects of life demand large portions of a man's time. In order to provide for the family, Dad often works long hours. Being active in his church calls for time to be spent away from home at meetings, prayer groups, and such. In order to stay physically fit, he needs to spend time exercising. His wife needs his attention, as do his parents. There is never enough time to go around.

Adults understand this, but most kids don't.

During one of Russell's teen years, Randy worked unusually long days. Many evenings his car didn't pull into our driveway until nine or ten o'clock at night—sometimes even later. We all missed him terribly during that year, but those hours that he was gone were especially hard on Russell. Every evening he and I would have the same exact conversation.

"What time'd dad think he'd be home?" Russell would ask.

"Ten. Maybe ten-thirty."

"How come so late? What did he have to do? He'll be home before then, won't he? Did Dad actually *tell* you that he wouldn't get home before ten? Did he *say* ten?"

I think that Russell wanted his dad home so badly that there was a part of him that held to the notion that if only he believed Randy was going to come home early, then maybe he would. He hated, *hated* those long nights without his dad.

Busy dads of today have to use creativity and flexibility in order to carve out time with their sons. Few fathers I know work from eight to five and come home at five-fifteen on the dot to spend the rest of the evening within their home's four walls. Families don't operate that way anymore. Most evenings, we are on the go in many different directions.

Yet boys still need time with their dads. Here are a handful of creative ways some fathers I know have incorporated regular time with their sons into busy, active lives.

1. Travel time. Families spend lots of time in the car. Occasionally let Mom sit in the back while a son (and when it's her turn, a daughter) sits in the

front with Dad. On an extended trip, ask your son to help out by looking up something on the map.

2. Chores. Boys who don't like working on their own will be inclined to do around-the-house jobs if they are helping Dad. When possible, pick jobs that require tandem effort such as moving furniture or building projects.

3. Breakfast out. During especially busy times, wake your son an hour earlier than you normally do. Even on a weekday morning the two of you will have plenty of time for pancakes and juice before you begin your work and school days.

4. Business trips. Depending on his age, his maturity, and the nature of your job, taking your son with you on your next trip out of town could provide both of you with a great time. Take along plenty of snacks, books, videos, and handheld games so that he can occupy himself while you're in meetings. Once work is over, the two of you can spend some quality time together away from Mom and his sisters.

Lessons in Life

A son learns much by simply observing how his dad lives, but there are some lessons he won't get unless Dad purposely sets out to teach them. Instructions about hard work, the proper way to treat women, the importance of good character, honesty, and honor have to be spoken out loud. A son needs to hear the stories of men in the family who have lived through hard times yet stayed true to their values and faith. He also needs to be aware of the lives of

those who did not behave in honorable ways and the consequences they and their families endured.

Dads, be on the lookout for teaching moments. Time
spent together in the car, especially when it's dark outside,
lends itself to thoughtful discussion. Occasions when you
and your son are walking or hiking together, playing golf,
washing the car, or competing at a board game are good
times to have talks.

Use events in the news as springboards for discussion.
Share situations you hear about that demonstrate a man
handling himself in honorable, selfless ways. Talk about
times in your own life when it was difficult to do the right
thing but you did it anyway. Share with him the goals you
have for him, for the family, for yourself. These discussions
don't have to be long, drawn out, and heavy. Better if they
aren't! There's no need to preach. Let even serious talk
occur in a relaxed way.

Look at Me, Dad!

Boys crave the attention and approval of their dads.
When they're little guys they don't hesitate to yell, "Hey,
Dad! Look! Watch me!" When they grow to be adolescents, they still want their dad to watch and approve of
their accomplishments, to cheer them on—even though
most of them are way too cool to admit it.

No matter what it is your son is interested in—sports,
music, drama, science, or art—praise his efforts. Cheer his
team. Attend his concert. Be there for his science fair. Brag
on him to your friends when you know he's listening.
When a dad gives his son attention and approval, he is
affirming his son's efforts at becoming a man.

Should he behave as if he doesn't care what his dad
thinks, don't believe it. That's a cover-up for a fear of failure.

Boys long to make their dads proud. They need to hear the message that if they've tried, they haven't failed. Boys crave the words, "Good job, son! You did great."

From Quarterback to Drum Major

My husky friend, Jeb, is a sports nut. He was a football star in high school and, except for a knee injury late in his senior year, might have gone on to play college ball, maybe even pro.

When Jeb was 20, he married Diane, who shortly after their third anniversary, gave birth to a son. Jeb was thrilled. Sam, the little guy in his arms, looked to have long legs and broad shoulders—the build of an athlete if ever there was one! Jeb began to dream of the day when his little boy would follow in his footsteps and perhaps even play college ball.

When Sam was a toddler, Jeb played with him every night on the floor. By the time he was two, Sam could throw a plastic football really well. "Look at that arm!" Jeb would exclaim. "Honey, did you see that? He can run too, can't you Sam? Here, Sam. Show Mommy how fast you can run!" Jeb would snatch his son up, tickle him, tease him, and toss him in the air.

When Sam got older, Jeb took him to high school, college, and even a couple of professional football games. Sam loved every minute of those games. Fascinated by football, by the third grade Sam could recite team rosters as well as individual players' positions and stats.

As Sam got older, Jeb was thrilled at his son's interest in watching games. He was less pleased with Sam's lack of interest when it came to playing the game. Small for his age and not possessed of an aggressive nature, Sam did not enjoy time on the field. Jeb worked with Sam to help him get better. He encouraged him to lift weights to gain strength and to drink protein shakes to bulk up a bit.

None of Jeb's efforts turned Sam into a football player.

Sam was in the eighth grade when he up and told his dad, "I don't want to play football next year. I tried it, and I don't like it. But don't worry, Dad. You'll still get to see me on the field when you go to games. Starting next year I'm going to play my trumpet in the marching band. We'll perform at every halftime."

Now what's a dad supposed to do when his son turns his back on something he loves, to embrace an interest that bores him to tears? If you're a dad like Jeb, you become president of the band booster club. You sell raffle tickets at work to raise money for the band. You chaperone band parties and you brag to your friends when your son, during his senior year, is awarded the position of drum major.

That's what you do because, like Jeb, you love your son and you know that his dreams are more important than yours.

That is exactly what you do.

> *The father of a righteous man has great joy;*
> *he who has a wise son delights in him.*

—PROVERBS 23:24

Doin' Stuff with Dad

1. Schedule regular times for Dad and son to have fun together. Working on projects, going to sporting events or concerts, or learning a new skill are great ways to build a relationship.

2. When planning an outing with your son, invite the son of a single mom to join you. Both boys will have fun, and a child who may not see as much of his own dad as he'd like will benefit from the time spent with you.

3. On Mother's Day, enlist the help of your son to make Mom a special breakfast. Make sure that when it's time to clean up, he's there to help too!

4. Plan a multigenerational, men-only camp out. Invite grandfathers, uncles, brothers, and male cousins. Enjoy the time together. Forget shaving and make it a rule that no one has to shower! Eat lots of fried food, go fishing, and stay up late playing dominos and telling tall tales.

15
Mama's Boy

"Goodnight, Mike. I love you."

"Love you too, Mom." Fourteen-year-old Mike ducked past his mother, Susan, on his way up to bed. So quick was Mike's maneuver, he managed to miss, yet again, the customary goodnight kiss on the cheek that his mom had given him almost every night since his birth.

Susan noticed. That made three times this week he had purposely avoided her lips. What was up with this kid of hers? Not only did Mike, a bright, communicative boy, suddenly not want a goodnight kiss, he had also begun avoiding her see-you-after-school morning goodbye hugs. Suddenly skittish about any physical contact with her, it had been weeks since he'd even so much as let her get close enough to lay her hand on his shoulder.

"Mike acting funny with you?" Susan finally asked her husband.

"Nope. No funnier than usual," he answered. "What do you mean?"

"Distant. Like he doesn't want to be touched."

Mike's dad had noticed nothing like that.

The next afternoon Mike was perched on a kitchen stool eating brownies, drinking milk, and reading the sports page. Susan, really bugged about this don't-touch-me stuff, decided that enough was enough.

"Mike. What's the deal?" she asked. "Lately you've been acting like you don't want me to touch you. Is there something wrong? Something we need to talk about?"

Mike put down the paper, swallowed, and pushed his glasses back up on his nose. "Mom, there's nothing wrong. We read about this in health class. Chapter 5 of our textbook. It's a natural process that every kid goes through. I thought you knew."

What? Susan scratched her head.

"It's puberty, Mom." His voice took on a knowing, authoritative tone. "When kids go through it, they pull away from their parent of the opposite sex and begin to identify with the parent that's the same sex as them."

This? From her 14-year-old son?

"Don't worry about it Mom. It's perfectly normal."

"Oh." Susan swallowed. "I guess that's, uh…good to know."

"When I'm in my late teens to early twenties you can expect us to be close again."

"I see," Susan said weakly.

"Got any more questions, Mom?" Mike gulped down the last swig of his milk.

"No. I don't think so. Thanks, I guess…uh, for the information, Mike."

"Any time. What's for dinner? Not chicken, I hope. Last night was gross."

Change in the Air

Few kids will be as open and articulate as Susan's son, Mike (who graduated from high school at 17 and is now off at college majoring in psychology), but most adolescents will, in their own unique ways, let their moms know that things between them have changed. Does this mean that as moms, we'll no longer be close, that our sons will no longer need us?

Absolutely not. No matter how old they get, boys still need their mothers. What they don't need *or want* is the same kind of all-encompassing involvement and control from their mothers that they've had up until this stage of their development. Pulling back from displays of physical affection from his mother is an early sign of a boy growing up. So is an increased need for privacy and a decrease in the number of open, easy conversations that occur between mothers and sons—which granted, is difficult, because it is now that we moms most feel like we need to be aware of what's going on with our sons.

Take a Different Approach

Boys this age will be more communicative if they don't feel forced to tell their mothers everything. It's not so much that these boys have stuff to hide; they're simply trying to establish themselves as separate from *both* parents, and especially separate from their mothers. They long for independence and respect.

The harder we try to make our adolescent sons stay little boys, close to us, dependent upon us, and in need of us, the more likely they are to push and rebel against us. By giving a son some space, by tolerating periods of silence and times spent behind a closed bedroom door, we communicate to our boys that we know they're growing up and that their doing so is okay by us.

A Tall Glass

When he was a toddler, Drew's parents noticed that their son was extremely sensitive to caffeine. He was a big talker who by nature had trouble staying on task, and caffeine caused him to chatter nonstop, forget stuff, race around, and basically make himself a pest. One or two glasses of either cola or iced tea was all it took to wire Drew for hours. It's no surprise that, early on, Drew's mother learned to monitor and severely limit his intake of beverages containing caffeine. Usually it wasn't a problem because Drew drank milk with his meals and juices for snacks.

One hot summer Saturday morning when Drew was ten years old, five of his dad's friends from work came over to help tear down an old garage that was falling down near the house. The men arrived early with the plan to stay all day, knock the structure down, and haul the scrap lumber off to the dump.

Drew, up early, was outside and working with the men from the first hour of their arrival. He'd always been a helpful, energetic kid, but even his dad was surprised and pleased at how hard Drew worked hauling lumber, picking up nails, and even shoveling debris. The other men noticed too.

Wiping sweat from his brow, one man said, "Son, you're doing a good job."

"This one's a hard worker," said another to Drew's dad.

"Working like a man, he is," added yet a third.

At their praise, Drew tried hard not to grin. Determined to work even harder, he cleared his throat, spit on the ground, and picked up yet another load of scrap wood.

When it was lunch time, Drew's mother called them all in. She'd prepared sandwiches, chips, cookies, and iced tea. In the kitchen Drew saw her pouring him a glass of milk. "I'll have tea, Mom," he said.

Tea was what all the men were having to drink.

"Drew?"

"Tea, Mom."

So she poured him a glass. Just like she poured for the men. Except that it *wasn't* a glass like she poured for them. For each *man* she poured tall glasses of tea. But not for Drew. At his place, his mother set a juice glass, one that held four ounces, tops.

"Here you go," she said.

Drew's face turned hot.

Only when Drew's dad gave her a look did his mother realize what she'd done. "Drew's worked hard this morning," he said. "Done as much as any of us. Worked as hard as a man. It's hot out there. Hot enough to make *all us men* thirsty. Really thirsty. Why don't you get Drew a bigger glass?"

Drew is a grown man now, a man with sons of his own. He doesn't even remember that day when his mother served him the too-small glass of tea. But she does. And it pains her still. "What was I thinking?" she laments. "I humiliated him in front of those men. Not that I meant to—but that's what I did. He was trying so hard to act grown up, and I treated him like a child."

Most of us will make a mess every bit as bad as the one that Drew's mother did. Without intending to, with our words or our actions, we'll embarrass, humiliate, and make sons feel put down.

I suppose it's no wonder that we moms have such a time remembering to treat our boys with dignity and respect. One minute they amaze us with their maturity and good sense. The next minute they behave like goofy little kids. It's hard to know if the son we're dealing with at the moment is the child or the almost-adult. We're bound to get it wrong lots of times. All we can do is the best that we can do. When our words come out wrong, it's appropriate to apologize and tell our sons we'll try to do better next time.

A Woman's Touch

Our sons will benefit from learning things from the feminine point of view. When he begins to see himself as a man, he'll be more open to our teaching him about how to relate to women.

Who better than a mom to teach a son how to act around girls? Point out to him ways that you like to be treated. Talk to him about what girls like and don't like. Explain to him the difference between what's acceptable behavior when he's with a bunch of his guy friends and the way he should handle himself around women and girls.

Though he's too young to date, it's during early adolescence that a boy will show signs of interest in the opposite sex. Especially if he has no sisters, girls will be a mystery to him. With good humor and a light touch, Mom can begin preparing him to someday be a good date and ultimately be a great husband.

No one can teach manners better than a mom. Mom's usually the best parent to take him to buy clothes and to help him figure out what to do with his hair. Guys need a few domestic skills, and Mom is the one who can best be his teacher. She's the one to show him how to do laundry, how to scrub a toilet, and how to make a meal. He'll love it when Mom says, "Son, all *men* need to know how to make scrambled eggs, bleach white socks, and write a thank-you note. It's time you learned!" If done with lots of laughter and even a bit of fun poked at the stereotypical differences between men and women, these times can help a son and a mom stay close.

But He's Taller than Me!

Dispensing discipline is my least favorite part of parenting. I suspect that I'm not alone.

The disciplining of an adolescent boy presents some new challenges—especially for Mom. It's not uncommon for a boy, one who prior to adolescence has been respectful and compliant, to wake up one day and begin bucking his mother's authority. He thinks he's almost grown, and he feels like he is hot stuff. Likely he's passed his mother in height and in weight, or he will very soon. Wisely, she's let him know she realizes he's becoming a young man.

Does any of this justify disrespectful behavior? Should it be tolerated?

No way! Parents are in authority over children—even children bigger than themselves. Stand firm. When your son challenges you, when he faces you toe-to-toe, don't back down. The way you handle his first assertions of perceived power can set the tone for the way he will behave toward you for the next ten years.

Sometimes it's appropriate to delay dealing with a situation. That's not giving in; that's being wise. If *either* of you is extremely angry or agitated over a situation, tell him you need time to cool off. Wait a few minutes or an hour and then talk it out and explain the consequences of his behavior.

Physical punishment, such as spanking, is inappropriate for boys this age. The removal of privileges is the method of discipline most parents use, and it usually works great. Time spent watching TV, talking on the telephone, playing video games, and hanging out with friends can be restricted should the situation merit.

Ideally, Dad will begin doling out more of the discipline as a boy gets older. However, it's not fair to expect him to do all of the dirty work. During a time when I was feeling exhausted, discouraged, and overwhelmed at the demands of parenting teens, I fell into the habit of asking Randy to tell our children things I wanted them to do or not do. And why not? It appeared to my tired self that they responded better to his requests than to mine—which of course made me feel even more discouraged and even incompetent. When this went on past the time of being reasonable, Randy finally said, "Annette, you're not being fair to me, to them, or to yourself. You are their parent too. It's not easy for either of us. You are not weak, and whether you think they do or not, these kids listen to you. It's your job to discipline Russell and Rachel when they need it. It's time for you to stop leaving it all to me."

Ouch. Randy was right. (I just hate it when that happens!) I tried to do better.

Actually, when we look at the way God ordered families, we see that the buck does stop with Dad. If a son is being testy and difficult to handle, the masculine firmness of his dad will likely be more effective than whatever his mother doles out. However, that in no way gives Mom permission to lay down her authority or to put all of the responsibility for disciplining on Dad.

Mother's Love

It starts the moment the little blue, hospital-wrapped bundle is placed in our arms. It doesn't end until one or the other of us is no more on this earth. We moms are head over heals in motherly love with our sons. When they hurt, our hearts break. When they're happy, we bubble over with joy. They drive us crazy with their noises and their smells, but they're so cute and endearing that, as we say in the South, we could *eat them with a spoon.*

Nobody is as special in a boy's life as his mother. How else do you explain big burly football players who mouth "Hi, Mom!" whenever a TV camera is shoved in their face? On Mother's Day, phone lines are jammed—and with what? Across-the-nation calls sons make to their moms. It has been said that injured soldiers, far away from home, always call for their mothers in the end.

Being a mom of an adolescent boy is a new experience—one unlike anything else. Yet the truth? When that lanky boy comes up from behind, wraps his arms around you, and maybe even tries to pick you up—there is nothing better in this world. Enjoy it.

Soon he will be grown.

But I have stilled and quieted my soul;
like a weaned child with its mother,
like a weaned child is my soul within me.

—PSALM 131:2

Time with Mom

1. Every few months do something fun—just the two of you. Take in a movie. Go skating or out to eat. If he's skittish about being seen out with you, invite another mom and her son to come along with you.

2. On his birthday, tell him about the day you found out he was to be born, and about how excited you were the first time you saw him. Kids never tire of hearing the story of their entrance into the family.

3. When he's had a tough week, surprise him with a treat under his pillow, such as candy, cookies, and a certificate good for one week of not having to take the garbage out.

4. When preparing for a car trip, ask him to bring along a few of his CDs—ones that you both enjoy. Ask him questions about the artist or the group. Tell him which song you like best.

16
Preparing for Launch

Our task as parents is to work ourselves out of a job. The hopes and dreams we have for our boys are that they will grow up to be strong, independent, kind, faithful adult men. Already, even in our boys as young as ten years old, we see the signs of those dreams and desires coming to pass.

At least we do on *good* days!

Too soon, we realize, stinky, size 8-going-on-10 feet won't be resting under our table. There'll be a lot less laundry to do, and our grocery bill will drop like a rock in a pond. Sometimes we can't wait for the day he'll be grown. "Come on! Become a man," we say. But then he does. And it hits us that we can no longer bend over and kiss the top of his head.

When he's not looking, we weep at the loss.

The moms and dads with whom I talk, like me, often question their abilities to effectively parent their adolescent sons. Loving these guys? That's the easy part. It's the day-to-day rearing of them that is sometimes difficult, frustrating, and discouraging.

Parents wonder:

Why is he acting like this?

He used to be so sweet.

Are we doing the right thing by standing firm on this issue?

What about that one?

Are we doing something wrong? What?

Seems that as soon as we make it past one developmental hurdle, three more loom ahead.

If you are a parent who knows that sometimes you get it right, but way too often you mess up, and it bothers you—a lot—I've got some good news. Welcome. It's a big club.

A friend of mine recently told me she was having trouble with her oldest, most compliant, and most obedient child, a daughter. The girl was being terribly self-righteous, judgmental, and unforgiving about some mistakes made by her adolescent brother—mistakes that he had been punished for and for which he was suffering the serious consequences. Yet the daughter kept mouthing. She refused to get off her brother's back.

My friend, when she'd had enough, finally spoke to her oldest. "Honey," she said in a gentle, but "fed up to here" voice, "you are right. Your little brother blew it. Big time. He probably will again. But guess what? Sinners live in this house. Did you hear me? Sinners! We *all* mess up."

Yes, sinners live in our house. There are no perfect parents and no perfect sons. We do the best that we can. We make mistakes. So do our boys. Thankfully, kids are resilient. We parents can goof up tons of times, and they will still turn out all right. What's important is that, above all, our boys know that we love them—*no matter what.*

We love them when they're good.

We love them when they're bad.

Yes, even when they are *very* bad!

The words in this book were written to encourage you as a parent, to give you a few bits of information and a little insight, and to assure you that your son is normal and that you, his mom or his dad, are doing just fine.

Parenting your son is an awesome responsibility. But you can do it.

Have faith.

Pray.

Believe in him, and in Him.

God bless.

And may you live to see your son grow to be a fine, fine man.

Harvest House Helps You with Your Teen!

Help! My Little Girl's Growing Up
by Annette Smith

Moms with preteen or early-teen daughters deal with awkward questions, roller-coaster emotions, and dramatic physical changes. Annette shares personal anecdotes and biblical wisdom for handling body image issues, instilling responsibility, imparting spiritual hunger, and more.

The Backdoor to Your Teen's Heart
by Melissa Trevathan and Sissy Goff

This book is a reference and safe haven for parents, teachers, counselors, and youth ministers who seek new ways to connect with teens—and who welcome the chance to discover new things about themselves in the process.

The Treasure Inside Your Child
by Pam Farrel

From the mom of three comes wisdom and encouragement for parents. Innovative ideas for loving and nurturing special needs, strong-willed, and prodigal children. Motivational tools and games help readers unlock their child's unique gifts.

Other Harvest House Books by Annette Smith

Everyday Angels
Annette's touching stories and delightful characters come to life in these 27 tales of God-given moments of unexpected light and meaning in the midst of the everyday. Renews with life-affirming surprises.

The Whispers of Angels
A heartwarming collection of stories that will bring a smile of joy and a renewed perspective on life. Annette's book reminds readers that life is a journey to be celebrated. *Whispers* will delight anyone who enjoys great writing, touching stories, and rich spiritual truth.

Stories to Feed Your Soul
Readers will enjoy this vivid, funny, touching, and memorable collection of stories that reflect the compassion, and craziness of small town life. These gentle stories touch souls, bring smiles, and reveal God's tender mercy.